SO-BIH-900

Patient as Partner
The Cornerstone of Community Health Improvement

AONE Leadership Series

American Organization
of Nurse Executives

American Hospital Publishing, Inc.
An American Hospital Association Company
Chicago

ESKIND BIOMEDICAL LIBRARY

MAY 2 7 1998

VANDERBILT UNIVERSITY
NASHVILLE, TN 37232-8340

This publication is designed to provide accurate and authoritative information in regard to the subject matter covered. It is sold with the understanding that neither the author nor the publisher is engaged in rendering legal, accounting, or other professional service. If legal advice or other expert assistance is required, the services of a competent professional should be sought.

The views expressed in this publication are strictly those of the authors and do not necessarily represent official positions of the American Hospital Association.

AHA is a service mark of the American Hospital Association used under license by American Hospital Publishing, Inc.

©1997 by American Hospital Publishing, Inc., an American Hospital Association company. All rights reserved. No part of this publication may be reproduced, stored in a retrieval system, or transmitted, in any form or by any means, electronic, mechanical, photocopying, recording or otherwise, without the prior written permission of the publisher. Printed in the United States of America.

Library of Congress Cataloging-in-Publication Data

Patient as partner : the cornerstone of community health improvement /
    American Organization of Nurse Executives.
        p. cm. — (AONE leadership series)
    Includes bibliographical references.
        1. Patient participation.   I. American Organization of Nurse
    Executives.   II. Series.
        [DNLM: 1. Patient Participation.   2. Professional-Patient
    Relations.   3. Nursing Services—organization & administration—
    United States. WX 158.5 P297 1997]
    R727.42.P38   1997
    610.69'6—dc21
    DNLM/DLC   97-1280
    for Library of Congress   CIP

ISBN: 1-55648-200-0   Item Number: 054100

Discounts on bulk quantities of books published by American Hospital Publishing, Inc. (AHPI), are available to professional associations, special marketers, educators, trainers, and others. For details and discount information, contact American Hospital Publishing, Inc., Books Division, 737 North Michigan Avenue, Suite 700, Chicago, Illinois 60611-2615 (Fax: 312-951-8491).

Contents

About the Authors

Editor

Julianne M. Morath, MS, RN, is system vice president for quality and vice president for clinical care improvement for Allina Health System, Minnetonka, MN. She also has administrative responsibility for the oncology program at Abbott Northwestern Hospital and is a member of the executive staff. Ms. Morath has 23 years of experience as a patient care executive. She holds academic appointments at the University of Cincinnati, Brown University, and the University of Minnesota, among others. She has done extensive postgraduate work in organizational leadership. Ms. Morath is a frequent speaker on systems thinking, patient care delivery design, and topics related to quality and organizational learning.

Authors

Barbara Balik, RN, MS, is the patient care vice president at United Hospital, St. Paul. She has facilitated major redesign and other change activities to assure cross-functional team development in managed care environments. She has published and lectured on her experiences in consumer and employee empowerment, collaboration, trends in managed care, and the development of quality improvement cultures. Balik is currently a doctoral student at the University of Thomas in St. Paul, MN.

Marjorie Beyers, PhD, RN, FAAN, is the executive director of the American Organization of Nurse Executives, Chicago. Previously, Dr. Beyers was vice president, nursing and allied health systems, at Mercy Health Services, Farmington Hills, MI, where she provided leadership for systemwide nursing and allied health services. She has published extensively and consulted in the areas of nursing administration and quality issues in health care. In addition, Dr. Beyers has presented more than 200 lectures to hospitals, nursing schools, and professional organizations nationwide. She was the first recipient of the Roy Woodham Visiting Fellowship Award for research in the areas of financing, organization, and delivery of health services in multi-institutional systems.

Bryan Bushick, MD, MBA, is currently consulting emerging health care companies. Previously, he was system vice president, performance management and improvement, at Allina Health System. In this capacity, he led Allina's efforts to assess and improve its overall clinical and operational performance. The effort has included implementation of multiple sets of key indicators and a comprehensive customer feedback system. His experience with Allina is complemented by his current role as a senior examiner for the Malcolm Baldridge National Quality Award. Prior to the Allina systemwide position, Dr. Bushick maintained a series of senior management roles within Medica, an HMO with over 1 million members, which merged with HealthSpan Health System to form Allina in 1994. Before Medica, Dr. Bushick was a consultant with Towers Perrin, where he specialized in employer coalition purchasing initiatives and quality management. Both his medical and business training were obtained from the University of Pennsylvania.

Carole Huttner, RN, MA, is patient care vice president of Abbott Northwestern Hospital, Minneapolis. In this role she is responsible for nursing practice surrounding patient care for 612 staff beds, 1,500 full-time employees, and a budget of $105 million. In addition, Huttner is accountable for operations, program development, and continuous improvement in the areas of women's health, surgical services, anesthesia, and social service.

Robert Jeddeloh, MD, is currently director of clinical health improvement for Allina Health System. Dr. Jeddeloh's major accomplishments in recent years include participation in and leadership of the collaborative development of a clinic that delivers services to students in Andersen School, an elementary school in Minneapolis. The project is developing a new model for the financing of school health care and has been featured in such national publications as *Business Week* and the CBS evening news. Dr. Jeddeloh provides medical oversight and direction to the Allina Health System/Medica Health Plan's Medicaid program, which currently enrolls 75,000 individuals in a prepaid, capitated program throughout Minnesota. He was awarded a Bush Foundation Medical Fellowship in 1993. He graduated from the University of Minnesota Medical School and completed a residency in internal medicine at Abbott Northwestern Hospital.

Rickie L. Ressler, RN, BSN, is vice president of patient care, regional health services, of the Allina Health System. She previously served as the director of patient care services, River Falls Area Hospital in River Falls, WI, and director of nursing at Abbott Northwestern Hospital in Minneapolis.

Gordon M. Sprenger, MHA, is the executive officer of Allina Health System Corporation, an integrated health care system formed in 1993 by the affiliation of HealthSpan Health Systems and Medica. Mr. Sprenger has been a hospital administrator in the Twin Cities, and a national health care visionary for over 30 years. Sprenger is the immediate past-chairman of the American Hospital Association board of trustees. He is a member of the board of consultants of the Hospital Research & Development Institute and a member of the board of directors of Medtronic, Inc., St. Paul Companies, Inc., and the Bush Foundation.

Ann Watkins, RN, BSN, is the community operations leader for a group of five inpatient care units and the IV team at Abbott Northwestern Hospital at Allina. She facilitates a multidisciplinary leadership team that manages all aspects of care, professional practice, and operations for the medical surgical units. She also directly manages the medical/surgical/neurological intensive care unit.

Preface

In today's ever-changing health care environment, at least one thing is certain: The patient's role is integral to the care process. Health care professionals are now challenged to learn the science of patient and family participation in care. How we go about ensuring this participation requires thought, a willingness to change perspectives and attitudes, and the ability to develop approaches that fit both the human situation and the reasons for change. The fact is, the patient's role has changed, whether because of socioeconomic and political changes, changes particular to the health care field, or increasingly high-tech electronic communications. The patient's position is now that of partner, coconspirator, compatriot, collaborator, and, in some cases, colleague. Health professionals need to face the challenge of this new dynamic.

Traditionally, health care delivery has been structured around the clinical knowledge base: Physicians, nurses, therapists, and others decided what care was needed and the patient and family accepted these decisions without question. This scenario is changing to a new one. Now patients and families are seeking and gaining a voice in what health care options are available, from whom they are available, and which is preferable.

This book is timely. The authors deal directly with the issues of how health professionals must learn to work differently with patients, families, groups, and communities in the design, delivery, and evaluation of health care. The patient as partner is here to stay. Robert Jeddeloh acknowledges this change in chapter 1, showing how new patient–provider relationships are being negotiated, old boundaries are being dismantled, and new parameters are being forged in the midst of policy and economic issues surrounding health care. He also raises a significant issue in asking whether access issues could be substantially improved if health professionals reached out to connect with patients on a partnership basis.

In chapter 2, Carol Huttner and Rickie Ressler take concepts from the first chapter—the patient as a source of information and decision making—

and expand them to new dimensions. They explain how principles of service, partnership, collaboration, utility, and economy guide and encourage patient participation, providing a pragmatic way to approach change. They also help health professionals reconcile the traditional and emerging philosophies of the patient's relationship with the health care system and providers. The philosophy and relationships inherent in the science of clinical care are being subjected to constant change, necessitating continued learning on the part of practitioners.

Chapter 3 deals directly with this topic. The author, Bryan Bushick, addresses the variables involved in accepting patients as partners. The explanation of considerations for evaluating participation encourages learning about the process at the same time that it provides insights to how to find out if the partnership is working. The author points out that involving patients in their care is part of a new science that requires systematic study to expand and improve it. In this science, patient preferences are integral to the design and implementation of effective protocols, care plans, and ongoing health maintenance. The author's message is clear: Systematic and credible evaluation provides the necessary foundation for advancing knowledge about creating, using, and improving patient partnerships.

Partnering is not easy. In chapter 4, Barbara Balik points out some of the challenges in navigating the transition to the new patient partnerships. She offers a process approach to this journey that looks and feels comfortable to those accustomed to the nursing process approach. Beginning with assessment, the process takes the reader through the necessary fact finding to a risk position of trying to advance new partnerships. Many of the phrases Balik uses—*integration, coordination, patient champion*—are familiar to nurses but take on new meaning in this highly variable context of patient care. The author is realistic about the problems that can occur as providers learn to become partners, acknowledging the human factors that complicate engaging the patient as a partner.

The humanness of the patient experience is brought home by Julianne Morath in chapter 5. This chapter captures the essence of partnership in human terms and gives the reader direction for integrating partnership with the existing health care system. Respect for patient values and preferences, along with flexibility in discovering and effectively using alternatives, are two important themes in this chapter. They are used as a basis in looking at the process for establishing an organizational framework and environment that support partnerships.

In chapter 6, Ann Watkins presents in detail how patient–caregiver partnerships can improve an intensive care unit and how the creation of a vision statement written from the patient's perspective can enhance the practical and interpersonal functions of this area of care. Watkins details how philosophical and attitudinal barriers to change were overcome and explores how the new philosophical orientation influenced construction and design decisions.

In his highly personal epilogue, Gordon Sprenger argues passionately for redefinition of such key terms as *system* and *partnership*. He recognizes that even as an "insider" in the health care field, he has had difficulty securing systematic care for his own mother, and he also recognizes that patients and family members on the outside will face even greater difficulties in the current health care climate. The redefinitions Sprenger advocates are visionary, yet rooted in the successes of the past.

The content of this book illustrates that accepting patients as partners has moved well beyond the rhetorical stage. Health care professionals are being challenged to make such partnerships a reality, not only in day-to-day communication, but in the way they design, implement, and evaluate care and services.

Marjorie Beyers, PhD, RN, FAAN
Executive Director
American Organization of Nurse Executives
June 1997

Acknowledgments

All of the authors are indebted to Nancy Garner Ebert in the communications/PR department of Abbott Northwestern Hospital. The following individuals provided technical support in manuscript preparation: Carrie Husnik, Jan Sutherland, Michelle Fredrickson, Dorothy Babich, Carol Holmquist, and Anne-Marie Holst. Gordon Sprenger wishes to acknowledge the assistance of Mary L. Small, director, communications services, Allina Health System.

Introduction

The many variations of partnerships, relationships, and human negotiations we experience daily make the notion of "the patient as partner" a conundrum. It can be just another trite phrase or taken seriously as a new challenge to be met. There is no question that partnership has been a health care theme in many different iterations throughout time. There is also no question that interpretation of this theme has reached a new level of reality. No longer is it sufficient to say, "We believe the patients are partners" and move on with life as usual. Health care professionals are now challenged to demonstrate their commitment to that partnership.

What is at stake for patients and for health care providers? First, there is the clear issue of a fundamental identity of self and of roles and expectations. Traditionally, the perspective of the health care provider has been that of an expert. Physicians attend graduate school for 8 to 15 years, including residencies and practice experiences. Nurses are not far behind, with years in graduate school and in postgraduate and structured learning situations with "masters" and "mentors." The main role of the patient has been to select a physician, nurse, or other care provider and then cooperate with the prescribed care. The insurance company (for those who were insured) paid the bills. For the noninsured, the notion of patient as partner has been a moot point.

Health care reform, and the attendant initiatives to curb the rapid growth in care costs and to ensure basic coverage for everyone, have resulted in a different scenario. The playing field has changed. Patients are now more fully aware of the costs of their care and can no longer rely on insurance to cover all of their health care bills. One of the mainstream interventions emerging from the health care reform chaos is managed care. In fact, managed care methods have brought patients into the care environment as contributors or at least as front-line observers of health care benefits and costs. People are better informed about their benefits and conditions of access, payment, and coverage. The patient's decision is often whether or not to use the benefits. Increasingly, people who have refused to be boxed into decisions preselected by providers or insurers are looking for alternatives. In fact, finding effective alternatives to traditional care is part of the breakthrough leading to true patient participation.

At this time, participation has both an economic and a lifestyle connotation. In recent years, beliefs about health care have been undergoing profound changes. The mystique of third-party decisions on what is reimbursed is giving way to new perspectives on care. People are now asking, "What can I afford? Are there other ways to accomplish care goals?" Evidence of this new thinking is seen in the growth and acceptance of alternative therapies, a growth that changes the expectations both of health care professionals and of patients. Health care professionals have long carried the banner of trust, confidentiality, and expertise in their relationships with each other and with patients and families. Formerly, they performed their role by making decisions for patients, whereas now they must reshape this role by making sure that patients are part of the data collection, analysis, and decision making involved in care and treatment.

A new knowledge base is needed to prepare health professionals for involving patients in care as real partners. This knowledge base encompasses the whole spectrum of care delivery, from policy and design of health care systems and services, to the implementation and provision of care and the way in which care is regulated and evaluated. Meaningful change must take place in all of these arenas. Although change may begin gradually in one area, gradual and incremental change is a luxury we can ill afford in today's health care environment. Therefore, health care professional workers would serve the field and their patients well by stepping back and taking a long-term view of the critical nature of patient participation in care. One could begin to attack this issue at a number of different levels, such as:

1. The patient/family unit
2. A group of patients with similar needs
3. Patient populations by common need, such as age, disease, chronic condition, or risk factor
4. Patient populations by geographic location, such as residence, school, or church
5. The community, or people who live in a given environment

As illustrated by these five levels, any new knowledge for effective patient partnerships will have to be multifaceted and multidimensional because the basic elements (people) are complex and interrelated.

The American Organization of Nurse Executives is working on a new framework for the knowledge base that nurse executives will need as part of expanding their professional growth. Developing collaborative patient partnerships is one of the areas in expanding nursing knowledge. A variety of new competencies are needed to effectively partner with others for increased participation and care. To partner with the people on each of the five levels, nurses need to hone their skills in a variety of ways.

1. *The patient/family unit:* The nurse who works to involve patients and families in their care must ensure that they are involved in every aspect of the nursing process, that he or she listens to what they have to say, and that he or she respects their preferences and decisions regarding care.
2. *A group of patients with similar needs:* With these individuals, the nurse must know not only how to involve patients in their care, but also how to facilitate a group process so that group interaction becomes part of the intervention. In addition, when groups of patients with common needs come together, there has to be a distinction about what is common to everyone in the group and what continues to be specific.
3. *A patient population with a common need:* Working with an entire patient population brings nurses even further into the interactive realm of care delivery. In any given patient population, there are care needs that are common to all members, needs specific to selected sectors (identified by type of disease process, risk factor, age, and so on), and needs specific to individuals. Planning care for such a population requires finding the commonalities in order to address all needs most effectively.
4. *A patient population within a specific geographic area:* This type of patient population requires similar interventions to those already described. However, the population of a given geographic area has issues related to their interaction with the environment they share as residents, students, or workers. In addition, the various social structures in the area (schools, churches, synagogues, industry and businesses, or recreational clubs) affect the population's health and care.
5. *The community:* Health care provided to the community as a whole can be considered an extension of the care provided to the four preceding groups. When approached as a singular entity, *community* is the aggregate of cultures, social structures, resources, and demands for care of its members. Nurses must master ways to involve community members in designing and implementing care alternatives, because the strategies affect the whole.

This brief overview provides only a taste of the skills health professionals will need to develop and refine over the next several years. Without question, it is an oversimplification of the extent of the changes that will be needed. Other complex bodies of thought must be considered. The broadened scope of health care is associated with different types of issues related to patient partnerships. Recently, traditional health care interventions have been expanded to focus on prevention, wellness, and health promotion while continuing to recognize the dynamic science of chronic care, risk identification and prevention, acute care, and care of the dying. Specialized knowledge applies to appropriate ways to involve patients in decision making related to each of these areas.

Much work needs to be accomplished to achieve the vision of involving patients and families, communities, and other groups in care. Health care professionals are challenged to create a holistic set of interventions that meet the demands of a widely diverse and ever-changing set of requirements. We are well on our way, and this book, prepared by experts in the field, gives us more than a head start.

Chapter 1 ═══════════════════════════════════

Establishing the Parameters for Patient Participation in Care Design, Delivery, and Evaluation

═══

Robert Jeddeloh, MD

Michael is a fourth-grade student with asthma, living in the Phillips neighborhood of south Minneapolis. He caught the attention of his health plan, part of a large health system, when the plan examined its hospital and emergency department claims related to the diagnosis of asthma. A six-month claims history showed that Michael had 14 emergency department visits and four hospitalizations with the diagnosis of asthma, no visits to a primary care clinic, and a widely erratic use of pharmaceuticals related to his condition. In a traditional model of health care delivery, this child and his family could be labeled "noncompliant" and "high utilizers" with all the values those terms imply: "bad patient," "bad family," and "bad part of town."

In an emerging framework of "patient as partner" in health care delivery, however, Michael and his family become a wealth of information. No longer "bad," they are a source of discovery: Why does health care delivery in their neighborhood not match acceptable standards of care for asthma? Why does this family not use a primary care office? Why are they isolated from the formal channels of information and education from physicians and other professionals? What informal social and community networks exist, and how can they be accessed to make information and education available? Does this family's isolation from formal health care and education represent a question of their "access" to health care? Or is the problem really the health care system's lack of access, its inability to reach out and connect with this family and the community in which it lives?

The Health Care Context

National and state health care reform efforts have fueled a rush toward mergers and consolidations for a variety of purposes, among them the desire to create economies of scale and develop the ability to produce measurable health outcomes.[1] Hospitals are closing, merging, joining "care systems" and

1

"integrated health care systems" that link them to physicians, and uniting with health plans so they can integrate and streamline care.

A key strategy of successful systems under increasing pressure from purchasers (employers and government) and consumers (patients and health plan members) is the focus on primary and preventive care as a principal organizing structure.[2] As financial restrictions increase, these systems will be under even greater pressure to incorporate primary care and prevention into business strategies. They will be faced with the necessity of identifying and addressing the nonfinancial barriers to care. Some examples of these barriers include the inability to gain access to a primary care site because of geography, lack of transportation, language barriers that inhibit education and learning, lack of accessible clinic hours, and lack of a "service attitude" in office and hospital personnel that makes people feel uncomfortable and unwelcome. Attitudes, such as the fear of cancer detection that keeps women from having Pap smears and mammograms, are another barrier to care.

Health care systems will need to search out and rapidly learn how to implement effective programs that target defined populations and identified clinical priorities. What determines these clinical priorities, who defines them, what defines an effective program, and who in the system is responsible for responding to the strategic pressure with successful implementation plans are as yet unanswered questions.

As health care systems are increasingly held accountable, the role of the individual health care worker on the front line of care delivery is still unclear. The rate of change and growth in health care systems has created the need for a workforce armed with new knowledge, skills, and attitudes to successfully implement change. The basic clinical knowledge and skills learned in medical school, nursing school, and other training venues are no longer enough to enable health care workers to cope with continuous quality improvement, reengineering, downsizing, and all the "movements" that speak to an organization's or a system's growth and survival.

To date, health care systems have largely focused on the mix, training, and distribution of primary care providers. Large systems have yet to examine and understand the variety of cultures, languages, and health beliefs their patients and communities bring with them.[3] Many questions are yet to be answered: What information do health care systems need in order to develop primary and preventive care structures that are effective for different populations? Where can they find that information? What can individual health care workers do to search out that information and implement it effectively to improve the health of their patients? In the rush to compete and learn the newest business strategy, the value of the information offered by a single child and his family trying to cope with asthma is often overlooked.

The Partnership

Each patient lives in a social and cultural context that creates and supports the norms for behavior that affect health, what it means to be ill or healthy, and how to cope with and manage a chronic disease. In this context, each person, whether consciously or not, has made certain choices: nutrition, exercise, use of tobacco and alcohol, the choice of jobs. Each choice has influenced the individual's and the family's health.

To be effective, strategies in health care delivery, primary care, and prevention demand that health care professionals have the knowledge and skills to learn about and help shape health behavior. Each person traditionally identified as a patient presents the opportunity for partnership and opens the door to another community and cultural context.

The word *partnership* encompasses a number of meanings. It incorporates elements such as relationship, reciprocity, sharing, equality, friendship, and participation. In the journal *Nursing Standard,* S. Wade writes that a partnership in the context of caregiving implies patient-centered care that includes patient autonomy and patient empowerment.[4] The business world has another meaning for *partnership.* Partners enter into an enterprise, and each has various responsibilities and accountabilities. The partners develop an agreement or a contract based on mutual goals and the need to support each other to increase their chances of mutual success. Intermediaries, often lawyers, act to expedite the relationship through negotiation, consensus, compromise, and, above all, communication. Each partnership crafts itself to match the characteristics, goals, hopes, and aspirations of the partners.

A definition of partnership borrowed from M. Winer and K. Ray's *Collaboration Handbook* describes "a mutually beneficial and well-defined relationship entered into by two or more (people) organizations to achieve results they are more likely to achieve together than alone."[5] The terms "patient-centered care," "customer focus," and "community care networks" speak to the emerging importance of the patient, family, and community as partners in care.

The current relationship between health care workers and their patients is often unequal. In a familiar scenario, the patient enters the hospital through the emergency department, feeling vulnerable, sick, and often helpless. The hospital environment, professional roles, and unfamiliar technology signal the rules the patient must follow to recover and return home. The patient and family are expected to follow instructions, take medications, and report back for follow-up care, usually to a clinic or an office that may be located somewhere other than the hospital. This relationship demands knowledge and skill from the health care worker and self-management on the part of the patient. Any sense of partnership in care exists almost solely among health care professionals, rather than with their patients.

What patients define as "caring" in surveys or personal reports is emerging as vastly different from what health care experts and providers understand it to be. In general, patients report that the existing structure and focus of a hospital interferes with meeting their needs, particularly with regard to making the transition from hospital to home. They also define quality in terms of care coordination and relationships rather than in terms of competence, technology, or efficacy, as hospitals often do.[6] The concept of self-management, combined with appropriate health care education, represents an orientation toward disease that works well for middle-class, Western culture and the health professions, but is alien to many others. Awareness of the differences in cultural perspectives or community norms should prompt efforts to understand self-management and partnership from the perspective of patients who may not initially see or value their benefits.[7]

In a climate where the views, values, beliefs, and expectations of patients are sought, health care professionals have a duty to listen closely.[8] To craft a partnership that is mutually beneficial and well defined and that accomplishes mutually agreed-on results requires that health care workers stop, get the lay of the land in terms of issues facing them and their patients, and take deliberate steps to listen to what their partners—their patients—have to say.

Listening is perhaps the single most applicable skill in building the partnership. It demonstrates respect and creates a basis for connection. It does not necessarily lead to action, but it can lead to knowledge and understanding. Posing questions and listening to the responses forms the basis for the level of communication needed to structure a partnership. This structure, or agreement on which the partnership is built, can be called a contract. The word *contract* refers to a clearly stated, typically documented, agreement between various parties. Often used to refer to a legally binding agreement, the word can also refer to less formal commitments, as in a "social contract." In establishing a partnership, the term refers to the ability to establish clear goals and to communicate directly and concretely about the responsibilities and actions the partners can expect of each other as they pursue the achievement of results.

Before the process of contracting can begin, it is necessary to arrive at a common understanding of a presenting problem and its root causes, or the importance of a presenting opportunity. The following questions may guide such a discussion:

- What information/documentation exists about the current situation?
- Who are the people in the best position to shed light on the cause of the problem/opportunity?
- What questions need to be asked to help understand the situation?
- Why is this problem/opportunity important?
- What consequences make this situation urgent to address?
- What are the short- and long-term implications?

The result of the initial discussion might reveal the need to collect more information, or, if enough is available, a problem or opportunity statement— a vision—can be formulated based on the question: *Where are we today, and where do we want to be at some time in the future?* When the answers to these questions are clearly understood and agreed on by the parties involved, three primary contracting areas can be addressed: (1) objectives or results; (2) actions, decisions, and follow-up (reinforcement); and (3) roles and responsibilities.[9]

The discussion and negotiations involved in contracting, exploring the needs and wants of the concerned parties, even the simple one-on-one relationship between the health care professional and patient, constitute a time-consuming effort that flies in the face of the speed and pressure associated with health care change. The time necessary to listen to and negotiate with emerging partners, especially if they are exploring new ways of relating to each other, will be a new tension-filled experience for those feeling the business pressures of health care. Arriving at a successful partnership demands time to sort out what is culturally appropriate, formulate a common vision, and develop a mutually beneficial action plan.

Partners by Design: From Patient to Community

The partnership forged between one health care professional and one patient is the essential component in building strategic partnerships with communities. The lives of individual patients are not normally marked by illness, and they do not live within hospitals and health care systems on a day-to-day basis. Crafting a partnership that values what patients bring to the health care relationship means moving away from the institution to learn the cultural context in which people live and make decisions. The communities where patients live offer a wealth of information.

Communities have formal and informal networks that offer mutual support and assistance, frame beliefs, disseminate information, and constitute the framework in which people live their daily lives. Through community organization, people develop programs that meet their particular needs, encourage them to assist and support each others' efforts, and help them gain further assistance and support from other formal and informal social structures and organizations. The community frames the context by which people feel encouraged or comfortable accessing other systems such as health care.

Once they are away from the organization, health care professionals can discover the elements of the community that may come together to forge a partnership. Successful partnerships involve grassroots, minority, and end-user groups (such as community residents, the poor and uninsured, and those with chronic diseases, respectively). This can be difficult when the initiators of the partnerships are from the mainstream (the hospital, public health services, and so on). Such initiators can attract individuals to these groups by making personal contacts, building relationships, and making sure that participation truly benefits them.[10]

The Neighborhood Asthma Coalition, a partnership between Washington University and the Grace Hill Neighborhood in St. Louis, is a community organization approach to promoting the basic understanding of asthma and encouraging improved care within four low-income, predominantly African-American neighborhoods in St. Louis. This coalition emphasizes strategies and social support through neighborhood and community organizations to reach children with asthma, their parents or caretakers, and other family members and friends.[11]

The Neighborhood Asthma Coalition represents a new paradigm of patient partnership. In this case, the health care partner, Washington University, recognized the need to move into the community—the cultural context of its patients—to affect one particular disease, asthma. The health care partner used its data on the prevalence of asthma, its incidence, the number of emergency department visits and hospital admissions related to asthma, and the overall cost of asthma care. It defined a problem with which it needed help. Armed with information, the health care partner recognized that a strategy for primary care and prevention required a new way of doing business. Research and the literature outlined particular strategies and pointed the way to search out new partners. Individual health care professionals initiated and built personal relationships with community leaders, church groups, families, and political organizations to facilitate the process. The health care system used its resources in designing, planning, grant writing, and human resources to initiate and nurture a collaboration with mutually defined relationships that could achieve a common goal: improved asthma care for children.

Washington University health care professionals recognized the need to work within existing community organizations and listen to what members had to say about engaging residents in successful partnership. The description of the Neighborhood Asthma Coalition's success, presented succinctly in the October 1994 issue of *Chest,* does not detail the time spent and work involved in establishing relationships, planning, engaging and communicating with residents, addressing and resolving conflict, or the nurturing required in building this partnership.

Winer and Ray describe the process of building collaboration or partnerships through the metaphor of a journey, a destination toward which travelers move together on a road they build. The destination is results, the travelers are the partnering organizations, and the road is the building of well-defined relationships and the accomplishment of mutually beneficial work.[12]

As a conceptual framework, collaboration supports certain ways of interrelating. "Cooperation" and "coordination" are different types of relationships and are the ways in which health care organizations relate most frequently and most comfortably with people and organizations. However, they fall short of collaboration and partnership. Consider the following terms and definitions:

- *Cooperation:* This short-term, informal relationship exists without any clearly defined mission, structure, or planning effort. Cooperative partners share information only about the subject at hand. Each retains authority and keeps resources separate so virtually no risk exists.
- *Coordination:* Formal relationships and shared missions may involve people in a coordinated effort to focus their long-term interactions around a specific effort or program. Coordination requires planning and a division of roles, and it can open communication channels between organizations. Although authority still rests with individual organizations, everyone's risk increases. Power becomes an issue, resources are made available to participants, and rewards are shared.
- *Collaboration:* With collaboration, a durable and pervasive relationship develops — a partnership. Participants bring separate organizations or backgrounds together to form a new structure with full commitment to a common mission. The relationship requires comprehensive planning and well-defined communication channels. The collaborative structure determines authority, and risk is much greater because each partner contributes resources and reputation. Power is an issue and can be unequal. Partners pool or jointly secure resources and share rewards.

Clearly, the journey along the continuum from cooperation to collaboration involves increasing levels of risk, committed time, and opportunity for all participants.[13]

Choosing Partners

Information about what is important to patients and their communities comes from multiple sources. The patient entering the delivery system provides the first glimpse. Health care information systems can augment public health data sources and allow caregivers to make generalizations and identify health care issues particular populations face. In most cases, there are very few surprises: Heart disease, diabetes, cancer, asthma, and high-risk pregnancy are all familiar to most systems. Health risk behaviors that can contribute to these conditions also provide no surprises: tobacco use, poor nutrition, obesity, and lack of exercise. Naming the behaviors is easy, the puzzle is how to affect, change, or modify them. To solve that puzzle, health care systems need help. Partnerships formed by patients and the communities in which they live, with individual providers and the organizations in which they work, can start to define and put together the pieces of this puzzle. The partnership becomes the strategy.

The Neighborhood Asthma Coalition resulted from the question posed by health care professionals: how to improve asthma care. From a different direction, residents of the Phillips community and members of the Family Resource Center at Andersen School in Minneapolis targeted four health plans as partners to redesign health care delivery for students and their families in this elementary school setting.[14] The community residents and teachers wondered how to improve children's health and began the task of engaging health care systems. The community started the journey toward collaboration. Again, asthma became the clinical focus. Each of these two partnerships negotiated and shaped a common vision of improved health care for children and developed the contract that structured their working relationship.

For a health care professional to reach out to a community and engage individuals and organizations requires time, patience, and courage. He or she is often in foreign territory. Agendas may be different, community politics may be frightening, and individual and organizational strategies that work well inside the health care organization may not work at all in community groups. Initial contacts may prove unsuccessful. The first people and groups that come to mind may not be the right ones to shape the vision and accomplish the work of the partnership. Established leaders in a community may already have a full agenda. Their eagerness to welcome a new health care partner may mask an unwillingness to shape a vision different than the one they have already established. To sort through the different people involved, meet with them, arrive at a common vision, agree to work together, and develop a joint action plan takes time and patience. Courage is needed to select some people, leave others out, move beyond the politically acceptable, and stay focused.

A mainstream health care institution may have difficulty accessing community groups. Its motives may be suspect. The usual pace of the institution will most likely be too fast; expecting the same speed in decision making from community partners can create a sense of mistrust. The individual provider who takes the time, pays attention, and listens carefully to community residents can build a series of personal relationships that contribute to building a strong sense of trust.

Evaluation and the Partnership

Once the contacts have been made, the relationships established, the agreements forged, the action plans developed, and the necessary group dynamics tested and shaped, the excitement of implementation begins. Pilot tests, programs, and action can capture the partners' imaginations and attract new participants. Andersen School celebrated the opening of its new health center with fanfare and a palpable spirit of joy and accomplishment. This partnership now moves to the next phase: targeted interventions and proving through measurement and evaluation that the health center is fulfilling its vision of improving the health care of Andersen students and their families. Each member of the partnership now seeks information in the form of ongoing evaluation to convince each other and themselves that the health center is a success.[15]

Evaluation is the feedback mechanism that keeps a partnership on track, true to its vision. (See chapter 3.) Evaluation can play an important formative function, providing a way to examine the ongoing implementation effort and identify the need for any change in direction.[16] This feedback bolsters the confidence of the people working together. The health care partner often has access to the expertise necessary to structure an evaluation process and assemble information in ways that make sense to the other partners. Surveys, both of the participating partners and of community residents, are one source of information. Utilization data from a health plan partner or a delivery site's database can be useful for ongoing measurement. Measurement helps the partners answer the questions: Are we on track? Are we making a difference? Are we succeeding?

The Home Front

Practitioners who learn to work effectively in communities cannot lose sight of the dynamics back in the rapidly changing world of health care systems and hospitals. The pace and timing of working with community residents, patients, and their families is different from the business life of the organization. Products in the form of measurable results will take time to produce. Return on investment, cost-effectiveness, and cost–benefit are familiar business concepts that are sometimes foreign to community leaders and residents. Yet these concepts need to be taken into account in translating the partnership's work to health care administrators and business leaders. These leaders will need special attention, information, and communication to help them keep abreast of the goals and accomplishments of the partnership.

Successful integration of community-based primary care and prevention programs into the business strategy of the organization will take deliberate planning. Several years may be needed to build the collaborative effort and mount effective pilot tests and programs. Administrators and business leaders tend to become impatient for short-term evidence of progress, so each success needs to be effectively communicated. The evaluation and measurement systems the partnership develops can provide necessary information — the facts and figures business leaders find useful. One example is a program for asthma care that redirects care and education away from the emergency department and in-hospital environment to the less costly setting of the home or school. This reduction in cost and utilization will appeal to health plans, but hospitals and emergency departments will see their business shrink. They will need to look at the results of the partnership within a different framework, that of improved asthma care and increased patient and community satisfaction. When the partnership can demonstrate improved care at reduced cost, the credibility of its work is guaranteed.

Funding: Operations or Charity

Even credible work needs funding. When a partnership has designed a program and needs funds for implementation, the search for money begins. A health care partner sometimes may be willing to provide up-front dollars for initial programs, but this is unusual. Partnerships can soon find themselves looking for their own sources of capital. Foundations and government grants are a primary source of funds for testing promising ideas and programs. In fact, federal, state, and local governments encourage and often require the formation of community partnerships as a requirement to obtain funds. Foundations have also shown interest in funding creative community collaboratives that include health care systems and can demonstrate improved patient-centered care delivery.[17]

Such resources can fund start-up and testing, but what happens after the initial stage? How does a successful pilot become "operations," a part of the organization's day-to-day business? Foundation funds and grants help develop a program and move it forward but can give it an organization-wide status different from and often less than routine, budgeted operations. Successful partnerships and collaborations may produce successful programs and yet wither and die without budget support.

A significant challenge for a health care organization is to enter into the partnership with the faith of success and the intention of integrating successful pilots into its budgeted business operations. Without that sense of faith and intention the organization is simply cooperating and coordinating rather than truly collaborating. Data and information are again important to prove the value of the partnership. Cost savings, improved care, and satisfaction all play a role. Early attention to the need for collecting the necessary data and demonstrating effectiveness is essential to move the work from planning, design, and pilot to a sustained effort for ongoing improvement. Incorporating the financial needs of successful pilots into the operating budgets of health care organizations is a prerequisite to success.

Conclusion

One child with asthma, one family trying to cope with asthma, and a health care system that looks at itself and acknowledges that there has to be a better way to provide care can actually create that better way. Health care workers can build on the skills they already have. They can listen to patients and families, and they can collect, analyze, and use the information they receive. They are poised to follow their patients into the community. With clear, common goals, they can join with their patients and design partnerships to develop and test new strategies of primary care and prevention. They can collect the information to prove the effectiveness of patient and community partnerships. The new partnerships can build systems that effectively reach community residents to help them make health behavior choices, manage their illnesses, and stay healthy.

References

1. Witmer, A., Seifer, S., Finocchio, L., and others. Community health workers: integral members of the health care work force. *American Journal of Health* 85(8):1055–58, Aug. 1995.

2. Witmer, Seifer, Finnocchio, and others. Community health workers, p. 1055.

3. Witmer, Seifer, Finnocchio, and others. Community health workers, p. 1055.

4. Wade, S. Partnership in care: a critical review. *Nursing Standard* 9(48):29–32, Aug. 1995.

5. Winer, M., and Ray, K. *Collaboration Handbook: Creating, Sustaining, and Enjoying the Journey.* St. Paul: Amherst H. Wilder Foundation, 1994, p. 24.

6. Koloroutis, M., and Miller, T. Intentional caring: an intervention for healing. *The Medical Journal of Allina* 5(4):31–33, Fall 1996.

7. Fisher, E., Sussman, L., Arfken, C., and others. Targeting high risk groups— neighborhood organization for pediatric asthma management in the Neighborhood Asthma Coalition. *Chest Supplement* 106(4):248–59, Oct. 1994.

8. Wade, Partnership in care, p. 32.

9. Block, P. *Flawless Consulting: A Guide to Getting Your Expertise Used.* San Diego: Pfeiffer, 1981.

10. Winer and Ray, *Collaboration Handbook,* p. 49.

11. Fisher, Targeting high risk groups, p. 248.

12. Winer and Ray, *Collaboration Handbook,* p. 26.

13. Winer and Ray, *Collaboration Handbook,* p. 22.

14. Lurie, N. *The Andersen School Health Center: A Proposal to the Allina Foundation.* Minneapolis: Allina Health System, Fall 1995.

15. Andersen Health Center Advisory Group. Minutes. Minneapolis: Andersen Health Center Advisory Group, Dec. 1996.

16. Connel, J., Kubisch, A., Schorr, L., and Weiss, C., editors. *New Approaches to Evaluating Community Initiatives: Concepts, Methods, and Contexts.* New York City: The Aspen Institute, 1995, p. 16.

17. Lafronza, V., and Berkowitz, B. *Turning Point: Collaborating for a New Century in Public Health. A Call for Letters of Intent.* Washington, DC: W. K. Kellogg Foundation, the Robert Wood Johnson Foundation. Seattle: University of Washington School of Public Health and Community Medicine, 1996.

Chapter 2

Creating an Organizational Framework to Support Patient Participation

Carol Huttner, RN, MA, and Rickie Ressler, RN, BSN

The health care industry is being reengineered across the United States. Pressures from third-party payers for more efficient care delivery demand that health care providers offer more for less. All over the country, nurse executives face the dilemma of balancing cost and high-quality patient outcomes. This challenge affords an opportunity to focus on patients and their needs in terms of both technology and the total care experience. This opportunity calls for a shift in delivery focus to one that includes patients as equals.

This chapter focuses on a framework that can be used in all organizations to make this shift. Work in this area needs to be grounded in five guiding principles: service, partnership, collaboration, utility, and economy. These principles are defined and addressed to provide a platform for further development. Examples are included from organizations that have focused on patient participation in strategic planning for the care continuum, and limitations of patient involvement due to cultural and ethnic barriers are identified. The chapter also explores patients' relationships with nurses and physicians.

Preparing for Change: A Strategic Focus

Organizing a hospital around patient care requirements means creating new models. New models may require remodeling or building new space. Or models can develop around such concepts as communities of care, which are based on an integrated team focus that says the patient is the reason we exist.

Philosophical and Guiding Principles That Invite Patient Participation

A number of guiding principles encourage us to invite patient participation in the health care process. These principles include:

- Service
- Partnership
- Collaboration
- Utility
- Economy

Service

A service orientation is one of the 10 major characteristics that bestow professional status on an occupation.[1] It has been defined as "a set of attitudes and behaviors that affect the quality of the interaction between hospital employees and patients (or more broadly, the staff of any organization and its customers)."[2,3] The implications of an increased service orientation for health care organizations include a direct impact on patient satisfaction that, in turn, positively affects patient retention, financial performance, and productivity, also reducing staff turnover and malpractice litigation.[4-6] Important consequences of patient satisfaction that have been documented in the literature include:

- *Increased likelihood of patients continuing to use a specific medical service:* For example, the patient exercises personal choice when he or she self-refers back to a specific service such as physical therapy, pharmacy, or home care agency.[7]
- *Increased likelihood of patients maintaining a relationship with a specific provider:* For example, the patient may continue to return for ongoing follow-up or preventive visits to the same primary care physician over time.[8]
- *Improved compliance with medical regimes:* For example, the patient is responsible for his or her own compliance with dietary guidelines or prescription regimes.[9]
- *Increased participation by patients in their own treatment:* For example, the patient not only follows recommendations of the physician but also seeks out additional information, questions their primary care provider in a positive way, or offers suggestions for implementing care recommendations. The patient may get involved with the decision between relying on a family member or using an outside home care agency.
- *Increased likelihood that patients will share important medical information with their provider:* For example, the patient may take initiative to share specifics about his or her history or family information that could have an impact on care.[10]

The potential for achieving these outcomes with the corresponding improvements in clinical quality makes it imperative that we embrace a service orientation as our professional responsibility. We must develop a greater understanding of those aspects of care that contribute to improved interaction between the provider and the patient, that is, the aspects that make a difference to the patient as they seek health care.

The integration of customer input and knowledge is a responsibility not only of individual providers but of nurse executive leadership and organizations as a whole. We must actively invite customer participation in our redesign efforts; our quality improvement efforts; and our strategic, clinical, environmental, and structural planning. At some institutions, this goal has been successfully accomplished through governing board interviews with community members, during which citizens are invited to sit on committees and task forces, participate in focus groups to obtain specific feedback for a project, and respond to surveys and questionnaires. The key to success in this area is the intention and commitment of organization leaders and staff to see through a new set of eyes. That is the real cultural change required of all professionals. We must recognize that our view of health care is extremely limited and that we need the perspective of community members to place health care and our delivery systems in the larger context of their lives.

Partnerships

Partnership refers to the coming together of various organizations to lend resources and expertise to a process.[11] Partnerships provide unique opportunities in the changing world of health care. If the intent is to improve the overall health of communities, we can no longer afford an isolated, competitive model. Local, regional, and national constituencies are demanding improved continuity of care among providers, as well as responsible resource utilization. The only way to achieve this task is through partnerships. These partnerships require that providers share ownership and accountability for processes that affect the health of the consumer and the community. We must seek out stakeholders and engage them in investing the time, expertise, and resources to create systems and processes that maximize limited resources. We can no longer afford the duplication and redundancy that have permeated our systems. The partnership model can help to eliminate multiple people or agencies working on the same project. An example is immunization. We currently have the state, schools, and a multitude of clinics and hospitals working on immunizations, and yet we have not done a good job of pulling these entities together.

A partnership model means forming unique relationships with different players.[12] New methods of interaction, higher level dialogue, stronger relationships, and new roles will be reflected in the kind of partnerships that will be required to meet the challenges of the future. Perhaps one of the most significant changes will be for caregivers to accept the patient as a full partner. It would be expected that all participants that come to the table would come as equal stakeholders with the commitment to participate equally in achieving a defined goal or outcome. A new set of skills on the part of our providers and managers is required, as well as a whole new perception of the patient's role and place in health care.

Collaboration

Collaboration is the sharing of knowledge to accomplish a specific process or task. In a collaboration there is recognition of a goals and outcomes common to all participants. Because of the complexity of health care, it requires the integrated knowledge that results from collaboration of those most involved in the work.[13] Only through the collaborative efforts of all health care providers within each community will we be able to develop innovative processes to strengthen delivery systems. Everyone must work together to identify, test, and implement best practices.

A broader definition of "health care provider" is required than ever before. Those who are really committed to improving the health of the community must be willing to take the steps necessary to understand and define opportunities for growth. An excellent example occurred in a rural community that had committed to decreasing the incidence of tobacco use in their youth. It was the involvement and collaboration of the community's convenience store owners, economic development commission, public health officials, city council, physician clinic, school system, and hospital that generated a supportive system that affected the entire community and was able to significantly reduce tobacco use in teens. The business community heard about the extensive use of tobacco by children. The city council brought their knowledge of legislation. Physicians described what they saw in the clinics. This kind of collaboration allows a system to actively partner with and affect an individual's health in a community.[14]

This new kind of community partnership significantly enhances the outcomes of a project. The ongoing collaboration created through partnerships allows all contributors to maximize their contributions to generate an outcome significantly greater than what any individual could accomplish alone. Finally, just as critical, are the learning opportunities and relationships that develop as a result of this process. They will be the catalysts for future, long-term community health improvement projects. We must do more than provide for integration and continuity across the entire health care delivery system. We must expand that system to include community members not previously involved in the health care process who may have more opportunity to affect the health of the community than those in more traditional health care roles. That would include schools, businesses, service clubs, volunteer groups, and politicians.

Utility

Perhaps one of the greatest challenges providers face in redesigning systems and processes is staying grounded in the reality of the work that must be accomplished. Too often we design systems and models based on the newest theory or broad global contexts. We must remember that health care systems represent extraordinary complexity, both internally and externally. The models we generate tend to simplify relationships and structures. In trying to provide a clear vision, we often neglect the step of retranslating the simplified visionary model back to a model that demonstrates the complexity and interconnection of structures and relationships. This step is essential to developing a successful, comprehensive model and assisting people in understanding the impact of the change.[15]

Economy

Economy includes the concepts of efficiency and effectiveness. To continue to survive in an environment of diminishing resources, we can no longer provide care from the same management perspective. This perspective is too limiting to achieve the economy that the future will require.

One utilization strategy that emphasizes supporting individuals in their use of health care and services is demand management. The primary goal of demand management is the appropriate use of medical care. Cost reductions result not from limiting or restricting the care that is given, but rather from reducing the demand for care as people develop greater self-care skills, knowledge, and confidence.[16]

Essential to demand management is moving the patient away from a position as passive participant toward the role of an active decision-making partner in the health care process. A paradigm shift is required for patients and for most providers and caregivers. Our paternalistic model has tended to insulate patients and families from decisions in which we have assumed they are either unable or unwilling to participate.

To encourage patients to participate in their care and make informed decisions that promote wellness and prevent illness, we have to look at new relationships between patients and providers that support this new paradigm. Critical to the success of implementing demand management in health care is patients' direct accessibility to information. Again, caregivers and providers must move from a gatekeeper role to a resource and collaborative problem-solving role in partnership with the patient.

There is a major opportunity for community involvement in the health care system. The creation of multiple points of access throughout the community for residents to obtain health care information is an example of how health care must be defined outside the walls of traditional clinic and hospital delivery sites. Clinics and screening centers could be set up in shopping malls, libraries, or near public parks or sports fields. These principles must form the basis for the development of strategic plans.

Adapting the Focus of Strategic Plans

The foundation of patient involvement is the creation of strategic plans that focus on patients and what they say they require. In the past, the focus has been on making technological improvements, increasing market share, and building bigger and better environments for care provision. Now it must include the requirements of the patient. This focus is strengthened when we invite patients to tell their stories, to partner with us through survey feedback, and to participate in focus groups. This feedback is then factored into the strategic planning process. For example, one organization used the Picker Institute patient survey information to identify specific 1997 strategic goals in the area of care transitions. Patients indicated in the survey that transitions are a major area of concern, because they have experienced fragmentation when going from primary care physician to specialist, or from hospital to home. Nurse executives listened to these concerns and commissioned a team to focus on improving continuity of care and monitoring progress in this area.

Governing Board Accountabilities to Listen to Patients

There are more than 7,000 health system and hospital boards in the United States, and more than 100,000 individuals serve on them. Boards are empowered by law to assume responsibility for an organization's affairs; represent its owners; and ensure that management, medical staff, and multidisciplinary staff further its mission and goals. Though the board has accountability, it is not able to perform the real work of the organization. Boards assume the ultimate accountability for ensuring high-quality patient care and must answer the question, Does our institution provide high-quality care, and how is that demonstrated?[17]

Bearing this question in mind, board members need to hear and see what patients and families are saying they require and have experienced. Anecdotal evidence is not enough. The stage for real partnership can be set through board retreats where patients strategically and intentionally share their experiences. This experience can be powerful for board members, who rarely step back from their focus on financial health and turn their attention to patients. Listening to patients and embracing and supporting their experiences are bound to lead to improved outcomes of care.

Understanding the patient satisfaction data, such as the information gathered in patient surveys conducted for Abbott Northwestern Hospital by the Picker Institute, helps to focus on building clear direction for improvement. The nurse executive has a key role in setting the stage for active patient participation at the board level.

Integrated Health Care Delivery That Involves Patients across the Continuum

Large integrated health care systems are forming across the United States. Whether they are nonprofit or for-profit organizations, they are focusing on patient care across the continuum. Patients are catapulted into systems in various stages of evolution that are having varying degrees of success at managing care across the continuum. Patients are demanding a seamless system that provides for continuity across the intersections and transition points.

The patient who ends up in a tertiary or quaternary setting may well be asking, "Does the right hand know what the left hand is doing?" Answering the same questions at every stop along the way and having redundant testing and paperwork adds to an expensive care delivery model that promotes little satisfaction for the patient.

A recent interregional study of cardiac patients demonstrates that they want care to be coordinated throughout their experience. The patients highlighted the following chief concerns:

- Long wait times for tests and procedures such as echocardiography and angiography
- Lack of continuity in nursing care from primary clinic/hospital to tertiary hospital, unit to unit within tertiary hospital, and transition back to local community
- Duplication of tests, especially on day of transfer from primary to tertiary setting[18]

G. Malone and D. Rudquist highlight two programs designed to strengthen the link between nurses and the community. The Hometown Nurse program links nurses in primary care referral communities with nurses at the tertiary care setting. This nursing partnership has increased continuity of care, alleviated patients' fears about being transferred to a tertiary care hospital by including nurses from their hometowns as participants in the care process, and increased the exchange of information and collaboration among nursing professionals. Nurse-to-Nurse Consultation provides a channel for nurses to formally share expertise and develop professional collaborative relationships. Both of these programs recognize the need for patient care to extend beyond the walls of the hospital, linking Abbott Northwestern Hospital in Minneapolis to referral community clinics and hospitals in greater Minnesota, western Wisconsin, and North and South Dakota.[19]

Factors to Consider in Shaping Interventions That Foster Patient Participation

Gone are the days when patients unquestioningly accepted the dictates of their physicians and other health care providers. There has been a quiet revolution in this country that has patients demanding the right to be active participants in matters surrounding their care. A plethora of multimedia information is available for those who know how to access what they want. Thirsty for knowledge and answers to their unique health care issues, they search the Internet. Here they gather information that they assimilate and bring to their physicians as they look for answers to their health care needs. How do we open our doors to welcome and embrace patient participation? How do we create working relationships between patients, nurses, and physicians?

Cultural and Ethnic Implications

We in health care have an accountability to understand and respect patients' values, preferences, and expressed needs. Though the disease state is described in physiological terminology, the experience of illness is a social and cultural phenomenon. Class, gender, and other social attributes determine how patients understand their illness, how they respond to illness, how they communicate about their illness to others, and how it affects their lives. Arriving at effective therapeutic strategies calls for a negotiated understanding between the culture of biomedicine and the patient's cultural experience of illness.

By hurdling the cultural barrier, we can foster an environment in which patients can participate and experience a better recovery. A pragmatic approach in caring for all patients who have diverse cultures and ethnic needs is described by Allshouse in his suggestions for improvement:

- Sponsor staff educational sessions around the ethnic and cultural needs of the communities served.
- Focus plans of care that reflect patient care requirements.
- Develop tools that elicit patient perceptions of their illness and expectations of their treatment.
- Develop standards for staff behavior to apply when dealing with ethnically diverse patient requirements.
- Teach staff to ask each patient what the patient's needs are and never to assume they know.
- Develop an environment that fosters patients' access to their medical records.
- Foster an environment that allows patients to control as much as they can of their care.
- Teach staff to ask patients how therapeutic decisions will affect their lives.
- Teach staff to negotiate therapeutic strategies with patients.

Patients' Relationships with Care Providers

The interactions between patients and health care providers determine the level of patient participation that can be achieved. Although this is true of all caregivers, this section focuses on the two primary relationships for any patient: those with physicians and nurses.

Nurse Relationships

With health care reform on the horizon, nurses are providing more services for patients, which may lead to enhanced patient expectations regarding access, cost, and quality.[20] Recently, the American Nurses Association conducted a study that estimates that 60 to 80 percent of primary and preventive care traditionally provided by physicians could be provided by advanced practice nurses at a reduced cost and with the same outcomes.[21]

As nurses provide more direct entry to health care, it becomes increasingly important to understand what patients expect from nurses. Matching patients' expectations of nursing care with that of their nurses has been demonstrated to be a major determinant of satisfaction with health care.[22]

F. Abdellah and E. Levine outline six nursing expectations that hospitalized patients have identified. They include rest and rehabilitation, elimination of dietary needs, personal hygiene, supportive care, reaction to therapy, and nurse contact.[23] Personal interactions between nurses and patients appear to be significant predictors of patient satisfaction.[24] In a study of hospitalized patients, L. Eriksen concluded there is an inverse relationship between patient satisfaction and the quality of nursing care as defined and measured by nurses.[25] Nurses tend to define and measure quality based on clinical indicators rather than interpersonal ones, but patient satisfaction improves as more interpersonal indicators are addressed.

The video *Through the Patient's Eyes* illustrates patients' firsthand thoughts on listening. Patients describe behaviors that make them feel like they are being heard and the great impact that nurses can have on patients when they take the time to listen to patients' views on their condition. The patients describe the need for nurses to move beyond the technical world and listen to their comments pertaining to the whole experience of care.[26]

M. Koloroutis and T. Miller indicate that patients expect their providers to be competent in their field of expertise and in the area of technology. Beyond that, patients want their treatment to reflect a caring experience.[27] Caring is defined by Julianne Morath as a commitment to protecting human dignity and safeguarding the values of humanity.[28]

B. Wesorick speaks to the independent realm of nursing practice being "services which enhance health by assessing, monitoring, detecting, diagnosing, and treating the human responses to health status or situation."[29] It is this realm of caring that forms the unique bond between nurse and patient. Nurses have an accountability to enter into relationships with their patients and "care" for them. This aspect of caring moves nurses from an institutionalized model to a professional model of practice. Nurse executives must support this aspect of care and recognize the healing powers that result when this bond is actualized.

Physician Relationships

Patient–physician relationships have historically assumed that the physician, acting in the best interest of the patient, is the one who directs and makes decisions about treatment options. The patient in this model should comply with physician orders and understand that a good patient never questions the physician's decisions.[30]

In the age of consumerism, this model is no longer viable. Patients want to be fully informed. Many studies indicate that, regardless of age, patients want to know the good and the bad news. They want relevant information which will help them make their decisions. Because patients report that too much information is overwhelming, providers must determine what information is relevant. In this area, what patients say they find most helpful is information regarding available alternatives, potential outcomes of the alternatives, costs, risks, benefits, and the value of each potential outcome. With this in mind, the physician has a role in providing understandable information so that patients can make informed decisions.[31] For example, a physician may tell a patient diagnosed with a cancerous rectal tumor about all of the available treatment options—such as surgery and its implications, conservative therapy, chemotherapy, and radiation—as well as the consequences of refusing treatment. The patient can then make an informed decision about the option he or she feels is most suitable.

J. Balant and W. Shelton look toward a patient–physician relationship that is based on mutual understanding in an evolving, caring, dynamic relationship that also includes the family.[32] The physician's first responsibility is to act as the patient's advocate for appropriate care with all other parties (social services, other providers, family members, and so on).

Structural Changes in Organizations That Foster Patient Participation

Global changes are needed to all facets of how care delivery is organized. There are a variety of ways to approach care and promote wellness within the organization and community, including patient-focused teams and communities of care.

From Hierarchy to Integrated Patient-Focused Teams

Each of our organizations has been built on a departmental model. Moving into the 21st century requires that we rethink this model as it fosters isolationism and competition. The new world view is that of a web, as described by Margaret Wheatley and Myron Kellner-Rogers.[33] S. Helgeson also describes this as a model in which leaders live in a connected, center-out, day-to-day style that forms a web of relationships and empowerment.[34] The leader is placed in the middle and helps connect the right departmental people around the work to be done.

With this forward-thinking approach, the nurse executive is positioned to transform the organization and break down boundaries and walls, bringing people together to focus on patient care requirements. This can best be accomplished through integrated strategic planning. This process focuses the entire organization on the interconnectedness of the work and provides the structure to radically reshape our focus on integration around patient care requirements.

R. C. Coile describes a move toward a model of integrated teams focused on managing patient care across the continuum.[35] The team will reflect more clinical expertise, with nurses and physicians playing a lead role in integrating clinical care and information systems. Highly developed skills in relationship building, facilitating, and networking will be necessary when leading the patient-focused team.

Communities of Care

Communities of care represent a new approach used by Abbott Northwestern Hospital as it seeks to bring integrated patient care teams together to refocus their efforts in providing care.[36] This 611-bed tertiary setting is organized around five "communities": medical/surgical and oncology; women's services; cardiovascular; neuroscience, orthopedics, transitional care and rehabilitation; and behavioral health. The other delivery sites organized into two communities of care are outpatient services and surgical services/anesthesia/recovery/preoperative care center. The last two communities interrelate to the first five as patients flow through the system.

This decentralized model brings nurses; physicians; quality management specialists; staffing coordinators; chaplains; and staff from social services, respiratory care, and environmental services together to focus on the care of patients across the continuum. Their purpose is to enhance the efficiency and effectiveness of the caregiving team and of patient outcomes. A direct reporting relationship of people in these groups to the community operations leaders helps focus integration of the work around patients. Tangential relationships exist with the practice boards or professional departments to ensure practice standards.

The newly formed communities allow the teams from each community to focus on five goals:

- Maximize staffing flexibility for variable volumes.
- Increase staff flexibility and support efficient staff utilization (cross-training in groups with similar skill sets/competencies); create more "whole" work.
- Realize common goals supported by aligned incentives.

• Increase the ability to manage patient needs across the continuum of care.
• Gain efficiencies through geographic proximities.

Ongoing monitoring of this new structure already reflects a more timely response to patient care issues and a greater sense of teamwork. For example, in the past, patients would wait up to six hours for discharge medications and education. In the streamlined process developed by the discharge process team, the waiting time has been reduced to less than one hour.

Physical Facility Changes That Promote Patient Participation

Over time, our health care facilities have focused on promoting internal efficiency, clinical effectiveness, and safety. Although these critical factors must remain intact, we must expand our focus to include the creation of an environment that supports healing and one in which satisfaction results in positive health care outcomes. We must commit our time and energy to developing a better understanding of how our physical environment affects the health care process.

J. Hutton and L. Richardson have coined the term "healthscapes" to describe the emotional, affective, cognitive, and physiologic impact of the physical health care environment. Their research suggests that the ambient conditions (temperature, air quality, music, colors, odors, lighting, and texture), space (crowding, equipment, furnishings, and layout), and signs and artifacts (signs, personal artifacts, style of decor, and way finding) all contribute to the internal cognitive, emotional, and physiological responses and behaviors of patients and staff. They also conclude that these internal responses and behaviors ultimately affect outcomes of quality, value, satisfaction, willingness to return, and willingness to recommend the institution to others.[37]

This focus on environment offers huge opportunities for nurse executives to participate and influence facility planning from a totally new perspective. It also provides exciting new areas for nursing research and study. The better we understand the impact of environment on successfully delivering care, on the promotion of health and healing, and on meeting patients' expectations, the more successful we can be at ensuring a positive health care experience for patients.

Lessons from the Field: Involving Patients and Families

In the process of creating a new intensive care unit, the multidisciplinary design team from a tertiary hospital worked with staff members and architects to plan a beautiful family lounge.[38] The open, airy feeling of the space was thought to fill a need for families. However, when the design team assembled a group of family members and asked for their feedback, they identified a different location which would better suit their needs. The families wanted to be inside the ICU, closer to their loved ones where they could observe what was happening in the patient care environment and be involved rather than set apart. (See chapter 6.)

The design team took that information and changed the location of the patient lounge in their plans. It has proved to be the right location, as family members comment on how well it fills their need for connecting to their loved ones. This decision, and hundreds of others that were made with feedback from patients and family during the unit's design, improved the quality of the finished facility.

Point-of-Care Service

For many years, patients have been shuttled and transported to diagnostic testing centers in the hospital and community. It's interesting to note the number of times a monitored patient has been disconnected from his monitor, put on portable packs, and wheeled in his bed for long distances, only to be hooked up to diagnostic machines that were on wheels! Those machines on wheels are now rolling to the patient so testing can occur in the patient's room. Including patients in the design of how diagnostic services are delivered has focused team efforts on the patient's needs instead of the department's needs. As a result, patient satisfaction has increased.[39]

Computer Support for Patient Participation and Involvement in Learning

Patients and families want to be involved in care decisions. From initial diagnosis to follow-up care, they are exposed to many settings, services, and staff members. Decisions surrounding what information is provided and how that information is shared with patients are a significant factor in the integration of services and coordination of care. For example, the delivery of patient education activities must be consistent, flexible, and interactive to meet ongoing and changing patient and family learning needs across the continuum of care. Patient education occurs at all points along the illness to wellness spectrum. Planning and available resources are necessary so education can occur in a timely manner at all points of patient contact: prehospitalization, admission, hospitalization, discharge planning, and transition back to the patient's community.

Health care organizations continue on their learning curve surrounding the use of computer-assisted patient education. Creative strategies are now available that allow patients with some chronic conditions to manage their care decisions and information needs via computer. For instance, a

CD-ROM program gives patients with diabetes information that reinforces discussions they have had with their physicians. They can review how to adjust insulin doses and plan meals, track glucose levels, analyze foods for nutritional values, and pace their own instructions about diabetes.

Another application of computer support for patient education is on-line computerized patient education libraries of information that care providers can access and customize for patients and families. The WAN PLAN (Wide Area Network–Patient Learning Access Network) is an example of an online document retrieval system that provides computerized patient education documents to a variety of diverse locations, such as physicians' offices, hospitals, clinics, and (through E-mail) homes and offices. Materials are consistent in format and content across the care continuum. With this system, medication instructions provided by the clinic practitioner, discharge nurse, and home care nurse are of identical quality, format, and content, and are easily available when they are needed. Other information resources such as diagnostic explanations, procedure preparations, or self-care instructions can also be accessed and printed as needed. Ultimately, these clear, consistent, accurate, and understandable patient education materials can be distributed at any time and place in the integrated care continuum at which patients are most ready to learn.

Linking Services in a Hotel Setting

Patients in tertiary settings frequently require treatment for long periods of time. During this time, they and their families are uprooted from their homes. On-site hotel accommodations at a low cost provide continuity, safety, and access to immediate health care. This facility can be used for a variety of patients, such as preterm, high-risk perinatal patients with twins, triplets, or quadruplets.

With decreasing length of stay for many patients, many hospitals have closed patient care units which can readily be opened for extended use by patients and their families. Hospitals that have attached accommodation facilities have developed day surgery programs that incorporate the use of such facilities the night before surgery. For example, patients scheduled to undergo open heart surgery can stay in the hospital the night before, decreasing length of stay and allowing them to spend additional time with loved ones. Family members can be close at hand during the hospitalization. Both patients and families report decreased anxiety with such an arrangement.

Recently, Abbott Northwestern had the tax status of its attached facility questioned by the city that wanted back taxes paid for a number of years of the facilities' service. The final outcome of a public hearing concluded that, indeed, this was not a for-profit facility like a hotel but rather was part of a service offered by the hospital to help patients and families cope with being away from home.[40]

Conclusion

As nurse executives, we have an accountability to model behavior within health care organizations that embrace patient participation in decisions surrounding their care. These principles—service, partnership, collaboration, utility, and economy—serve as a framework to encourage patient participation in health care.

As nurse executives develop strategic plans for the future, these principles serve as a source to guide that planning. The stage must be set to invite patient participation. Across the United States, there are numerous examples demonstrating improved patient experiences when patients directly participate in projects that ultimately affect them. Whether it is a new building project, renovation, system redesign, or implementation of new technology, the outcome can be enhanced if patients are listened to and their input acted on.

Listening to patients' needs as they experience care focuses our work on our professional obligation. We have to care for our patients and nurture collaborative relationships with them in order to help them heal.

References

1. Reed, R. R., and Evans, D. The deprofessionalization of medicine: causes, effects and responses. *JAMA* 258(22):3279–82, Dec. 11, 1987.

2. Hogan, J., Hogan, R., and Busch, C. M. How to measure service orientation. *Journal of Applied Psychology* 69(1):167–73, Feb. 1984.

3. O'Connor, S. J., and Shewchuk, R. Service quality revisited: striving for a new orientation. *Hospitals & Health Services Administration* 40(4):535–52, Winter 1995.

4. O'Connor, S. J., Shewchuk, R. M., and Bowers, M. R. A model of service quality perceptions and health care consumer behavior. *Journal of Hospital Marketing* 6(1):69–92, 1992.

5. Nelson, E. C., and others. Do patient perceptions of quality relate to hospital financial performance? *Journal of Health Care Marketing* pp. 6–13, Dec. 1992.

6. Brown, S. W., Bronkesh, S. J., Nelson, A., and Wood, S. D. *Patient Satisfaction Pays: Quality Service for Practice Success.* Gaithersburg, MD: Aspen, 1993.

7. Thomas, J. W., and Penchansky, R. Relating satisfaction with access to utilization of services. *Medical Care* 21(9):553–68, 1984.

8. Marquis, M. S. Patient satisfaction and change in medical care provider: a longitudinal study. *Medical Care* 21(8):821–29, 1983.

9. Wartman, S. A. Patient understanding and satisfaction as predictors of compliance. *Medical Care* 21(9):886–91, 1983.

10. Bartlett and others. The effects of physician communication skills on patient satisfaction, recall, and adherence. *Journal of Chronic Disease* 37(9/10):755–64, 1984.

11. Pike and others. A new architecture for quality assurance: nurse-physician collaboration. *The Journal of Nursing Care Quality* 7(3):1–8, Apr. 1993.

12. Porter-O'Grady, T. Building new partnerships at the point of care. *Nursing Administration Quarterly* 19(3):viii–x, 1995.

13. Wade, S. Partnership in care: a critical review. *Nursing Standard* 9(48), Aug. 1995.

14. Donahoe, B., Kohles, M. K., and Gillespie, K. B. Celebrating the journey: a final report. *Strengthening Hospital Nursing: A Program to Improve Patient Care.* St. Petersburg, FL: Robert Wood Johnson Foundation and Pew Charitable Trust, 1996.

15. Ashmos, D. P., Duchon, D., Hauge, F. E., and McDaniel, R. R. Internal complexity and environmental sensitivity in hospitals. *The Journal of the Foundation of the American College of Health Care Executives* 41(4):535–53, 1996.

16. Vickery, D. M., and Lynch, W. D. Demand management: enabling patients to use medical care appropriately. *Journal of Emergency Medicine* 37(5):551–57, 1995.

17. Pointer, D., and Ewell, C. Really governing: what type of work should boards be doing? *Hospitals and Health Services Administration* 40(3):316–31, 1995.

18. Abbott Northwestern Hospital, Minneapolis, and Health Bond, Mankato, MN. Patient centered redesign of interregional health care; a demonstration project with cardiovascular patients. Unpublished project, 1996.

19. Malone, G., and Rudquist, D. Abbott Northwestern Hospital final report to Robert Wood Johnson Foundation and Pew Charitable Trust. Unpublished report, 1996.

20. Nash, M. G., and others. Managing expectations between patient and nurse. *Journal of Nursing Administration* 24(11):49–55, 1994.

21. Sherer, J. L. Health care reform: nursing's vision of change. *Hospitals* 67(8):20–26, 1993.

22. Ross, C., Frommelt, G., Hazelwood, L., and Chang, R. The role of expectations in patient satisfaction with medical care. *Journal of Health Care Marketing* 7(4):16–26, 1987.

23. Abdellah, F., and Levine, E. Developing a measure of patient and personal satisfaction with nursing care. *Nursing Resource* (5):100–108, 1957.

24. Spitzer, R. B. Meeting consumer expectations. *Nursing Administration Quarterly* 12(3):31–39, 1988.

25. Eriksen, L. Patient satisfaction: an indicator of nursing care quality? *Nursing Management* 18(7):31–35, 1987.

26. The Picker Institute, producer. *Through the Patient's Eyes.* Video. Boston: The Picker Institute, 1995.

27. Koloroutis, M., and Miller, T. Intentional caring. *The Medical Journal of Allina* 7(4):31–33, 1996.

28. Morath, J. Nurse week: a celebration of the practice of nursing. *Nursing Update.* Minneapolis: Abbott Northwestern Hospital, May 1992.

29. Wesorick, B. *A Journey from Old to New Thinking.* Grandville, MI: Grandville Printing Co., 1995, p. 110.

30. Deber, R. B. Physicians in health management: 8. The patient–physician partnership: decision making, problem solving, and the desire to participate. *Canadian Medical Association Journal* 151(4):423–27, 1996.

31. Deber, Physicians in health management, p. 425.

32. Balant, J., and Shelton, W. The patient–physician relationship: regaining the initiative. *JAMA* 275(11):887–91, 1996.

33. Wheatley, M. J. *Leadership and the New Science.* San Francisco: Berrett-Koehler, 1992.

34. Helgesen, S. *The Web of Inclusion.* New York City: Doubleday, 1995.

35. Coile, R. C. Management teams for the 21st century. *Health Care Executive* 11(1):36–41, 1996.

36. Abbott Northwestern Hospital, Minneapolis. Innovation steering committee report. Personal communication, 1996.

37. Hutton, J., and Richardson, L. Healthscapes: the role of the facility and physical environment on consumer attitudes, satisfaction, quality assessments, and behaviors. *Health Care Management Review* 20(2):48–61, 1995.

38. Watkins, A. Abbott Northwestern Hospital Final Report to Robert Wood Johnson Foundation and Pew Charitable Trust. Personal communication, 1996.

39. Donahoe, Kohles, and Gillespie, Celebrating the journey, p. 71.

40. Abbott Northwestern Hospital, Minneapolis. Report to President's Council. Personal communication, Nov. 1996.

Chapter 3

Considerations for Evaluation

Bryan Bushick, MD, MBA

There is little doubt that a shift toward increased patient participation has occurred in health care. The nursing and medical literature are full of references marking this transition, and the very nature of this book stands as evidence to the fact.[1-7] Though an accepted definition of participation is lacking, terms associated with this trend include *collaboration, partnership,* and *consumerism.* The focus on participation reflects a recognition and manifestation of the moral principle of patient autonomy. This orientation stands in contrast to the historical paternalistic orientation in medicine and to the principle of beneficence, in which the patient was expected to comply with and not question the physician's decision.[8] Although interpretations differ, health care providers, purchasers, and patients themselves support a more active role for patients. Some advocates, such as the World Health Organization, have gone so far as to describe participation as a duty born out of necessity.[9]

Benefits of participation are documented and often touted by advocates. However, studies are somewhat limited in number, and consideration of research subjects and methods is needed before making the generalization that the benefits of participation can be brought to the general population. Outcomes of care and patient compliance and satisfaction are among the areas found to be positively affected by patient participation.[10-14] However, one should also note that detrimental results, such as increased anxiety and frustration, as well as decreased satisfaction, have also been observed.[15,16] Regardless of the presence of favorable documentation, the fact remains that optimal treatment often depends on patient preferences and the values patients assign to various potential outcomes.[17] Clarity regarding such preferences can only be obtained by engaging patients in the process of care.

The inconsistency in previous research has extended to patients' desire to participate. Though some studies confirm that the general enthusiasm of many health professionals regarding the appropriateness of participation is often matched by patients who desire involvement, others document significant

31

reluctance among patients to play an active role in certain situations.[18-23] Given the lack of consensus regarding the definition of participation and the fact that many studies failed to provide specific definitions on which to base responses and observations, some researchers have questioned the meaning of much of the previous work in this area.[24-26] Along with S. E. Jewell, S. Waterworth and K. A. Luker have raised concerns regarding the "unreflective" practice of or commitment to patient participation among health care professionals and have noted the limited investigation of the concept of participation and its appropriateness for all patients.[27]

Despite the rising tide of support for patient participation from many sources, the specific definition of, patient desire for, and actual practices and benefits of participation remain ambiguous. Overall, research exploring this facet of health care delivery is limited, and further assessment of various factors is sorely needed. Opportunities exist to evaluate what patients want, what actually happens in the care process, and, when participation occurs, what impact it has. This chapter identifies and explains the considerations that should be taken into account when developing a system for such evaluation.

Patient Expectations

As with any aspect of health services, those within the industry must guard against assuming knowledge of patient expectations or, worse yet, proscribing solutions based on judgments of how patients *should* be treated and how they *should* act as recipients of care. Too often, health care approaches follow the assumptions maintained by clinicians and administrators and result in convenience to the providers of service rather than its recipients. J. Ende and colleagues reflect, "Not surprisingly, arguments for or against patient autonomy or physician paternalism, limited or otherwise, have been based principally on normative ethical reasoning without appropriate consideration of actual preferences."[28] True patient focus requires a commitment and investment to identify patient expectations. Research is specific enough if:

- Requirements have meaning and are interpretable
- Requirements can be confirmed and/or refined by patients over time
- Explicit prioritization can occur
- Providers and health care organizations can act on the expectations
- Evaluation methods can be designed and implemented

In keeping with the first consideration listed, if it assumed that a patient requirement involves participation, clear definitions are needed before any evaluation can occur regarding the nature of participation or its impact in a given situation. What is meant by *participation*? Is this term understood by and is the concept acceptable to patients and care providers? What are the objectives or anticipated benefits of patient participation? Although some of these questions might seem obvious, the literature suggests such basic considerations are often lacking even when champions of participation advocate its incorporation as clinical services are developed or redesigned. Responses to such questions provide the framework for evaluation.

An example of how requirements can be defined and applied is outlined in figure 3-1. Through increasingly specific definitions, meaning for and agreement on the general concept of participation can be reached. Staff are then able to identify work processes associated with fulfilling patient needs. Clarity also permits negotiation when the requirements of different customer segments are at odds or when health care providers and organizations are not prepared to deliver what is being sought by patients and their families.

The applicability of such an orientation is not limited to the issue of participation. In fact, countless instances in the quality and service excellence literature reinforce the vital practice of identifying and responding to customer requirements. The various techniques for gathering customer data are summarized elsewhere.[29-32]

Figure 3-1. Cascade for Defining and Applying Patient Participation Requirements

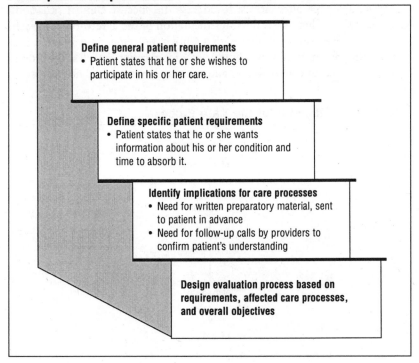

Define general patient requirements
- Patient states that he or she wishes to participate in his or her care.

Define specific patient requirements
- Patient states that he or she wants information about his or her condition and time to absorb it.

Identify implications for care processes
- Need for written preparatory material, sent to patient in advance
- Need for follow-up calls by providers to confirm patient's understanding

Design evaluation process based on requirements, affected care processes, and overall objectives

Primary Variables Affecting Participation

The intuitive appeal and presumed importance of participation overshadows its complexity. Multiple variables in three major areas—the care process, the patient, and the provider—influence both the process of participation and evaluation of its effectiveness.

The Care Process

By its nature, participation is relational, requiring interaction between the patient and others in the health care system. Too often, the concept is merged with that of the patient–provider relationship as if the two were the same. Figure 3-2 outlines points in the care process at which patient participation must be considered. These points are:

- *Information:* This step involves exchanging background information with the patient and assembling the facts surrounding his or her clinical situation (for example, patient data, disease background, alternative approaches).
- *Discussion:* At this point, the information is processed through dialogue with the patient and the objective data are supplemented with subjective input reflecting values, preferences, and biases.
- *Decision making:* This step entails the choice of a course of action, from among available alternatives, to address the specific clinical situation.
- *Intervention:* This step is the implementation of the agreed-on approach.
- *Evaluation:* As those familiar with quality improvement are aware, it is at this point that the results (outcomes) of the intervention as well as the process steps involved in care delivery (and the care environment) are assessed.

Figure 3-2. Elements of the Care Process

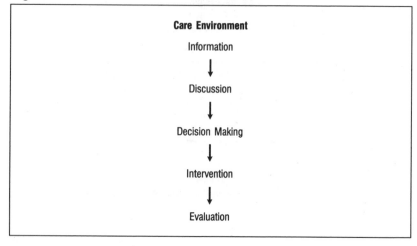

- *Care environment:* The setting and context within which the previous steps occur has a material impact. The same care process may have significantly different results in different environments.

It appears that many studies and advocates do not distinguish between these discrete steps. As an example, patients appear to have great interest in obtaining information about their condition and the options for proceeding, but less in actually assuming full decision-making responsibility.[33] This ambiguity is punctuated by the fact that preferences at different stages of the process are independent. That is, preference for information does not necessarily correlate with preference regarding decision making.

The first discrete step in the care process, provision of information, may offer the most promising foundation for progress in evaluating participation. Though patient preferences vary, it appears that a majority of patients do want to be informed.[34,35] Unfortunately, the clarity stops there. Little research has been done regarding the *types* of information needed by patients who assume a participatory role.[36] Additionally, although progress is occurring, there is still a significant limit to the medical information that can be disseminated regarding the efficacy and risks associated with many interventions. Considerations for providing information must include:

- *Content:* Factors including quantity, accuracy, and completeness must be incorporated into the development of communication materials to meet patient needs.
- *Timing:* Even the best material can be of limited value when delivered at an inopportune time. Clearly, numerous situations during the care experience affect patients' capacity to incorporate information and fully participate in care.
- *Method of delivery:* Thought must be given to implications for initial comprehension as well as future reference when establishing methods for delivering health care information. Developments involving information technology have greatly extended options (and even further complicated consideration of this aspect of communication). As an example, the shared decision-making program championed by J. F. Kasper, A. G. Mulley, and J. E. Wennberg uses interactive videodisc technology.[37,38]
- *Efficiency.* As with any element of health care, available resources are a major factor when planning for changes in process based on new principles.

Additionally, incorporation of patient values and preferences is often still needed before the information can be of maximal use to patients. Evaluation of the information stage should consider such issues as patient comprehension, patient perception of value, actual use by patients and other important stakeholders such as their families, correlation of information with other steps in the process and patient compliance, linkage with clinical outcomes, cost of various approaches, and recommended enhancements. Obviously, research into these areas requires focus and prioritization.

Referring to the care process outlined in figure 3-2, one should also note the step involving evaluation. Paradoxically, patient perspectives regarding their overall care experience are not routinely sought in settings where general participation in other aspects of care is fostered or even expected. This inconsistency must be addressed. The patient's voice in the evaluation of participation and clinical performance must be incorporated in existing monitoring and improvement activities. P. Reiley and colleagues remind us that, to improve care from the patient's perspective, the patient must be engaged in the effort.[39]

Further complications stem from the spectrum of possibilities for participation that exist at each step shown in figure 3-2. Rather than a simple binary interaction between physician and patient, a wide range of parties may play a role. This phenomenon is reinforced by literature suggesting an ideal state of shared decision making in which the patient and all providers play a role.[40–42]

Finally, it is critical that the context in which the interaction occurs—the care environment or setting—be taken into account. Environmental and attitudinal barriers can significantly impair the effectiveness of a participatory patient–provider relationship even when both individuals are fully interested and committed. For example, noise or other distractions in the care setting or unavailability of informational materials could limit meaningful participation.

Patient Variables

The issue of evaluation becomes more complicated when one considers the range of variables affecting patients' desire for a participatory role. Interest in participation is associated with the patient's age, education, cultural background, and presence of a significant other.[43,44] For example, younger adult patients tend to want (and expect) more voice in their care than older patients do. The degree of illness as well as the type of illness—acute or chronic—influence participation desires.[45,46] Patients maintain differing views when separating clinical care into its technical and interpersonal dimensions, although most are more apt to leave the highly technical issues and decisions to health professionals. Specificity regarding the types of choices with which patients desire involvement is lacking.[47] Finally, as if all of these factors were not confusing enough, the preferences of any given individual can change over time.

Although studies have identified these variables, proven associations between them and a patient's participatory preferences are weak. Preference varies based on individual, independent factors. Consequently, health care professionals cannot easily assign patients to participation-preference categories. Research has documented the limited accuracy of physician insight into patient preference.[48] Only direct conversation with patients will result in understanding their expectations regarding participation at any one time.

Provider Variables

Variables also exist on the provider side of the relationship. The complexity that health care professionals introduce is reflected by the roles and inter-relationships different professions maintain with patients. Relative to providing information, J. Ovretveit noted that interprofessional customs and disputes exist over which professions should provide which information.[49] Though both nurses and physicians may advocate participation, their roles in relating to the patient can vary dramatically based on the setting and context of the interaction (for example, an inpatient admission, a visit to a physician's office, a home visit). This reality is becoming more complicated as other types of caregivers are brought into regular contact with patients under the auspices of increasingly patient-focused care and other changes in the operations of health care organizations and clinical practices. A multitude of individuals now interface with the patient, bringing their own professional and personal perspectives and capabilities to support meaningful participation. H. S. Kim suggested some medical professionals are lagging behind the patient relative to information sharing and support of participation. Thus, changes in individual practitioners' fundamental beliefs regarding authority and self-determination will be necessary.[50]

Finding a Balance

Considering the complexity introduced by variables involving patients, providers, and the care environment, greater thought must be given to segmentation. Participation must be supported in those situations in which it is most desired by patients and in which it provides the most value, because resources are limited and the intricacies of providing health care services are considerable. We hope that research will confirm some universal patient requirements that can be used as a foundation for establishing standards for participation that extend across populations and clinical situations. Such standards could be regarded as a universal, or fixed, approach to participation. Conversely, individual patients' values, preferences, and clinical conditions must be considered in participatory relationships, necessitating a variable approach.

As illustrated in figure 3-3, the ideal is to establish a point of tension, or balance, between these two approaches. Such a balance cannot be found without the design and implementation of meaningful evaluation processes regarding patient participation.

**Figure 3-3. Balance of Universal and Variable Approaches
to Fostering Participation**

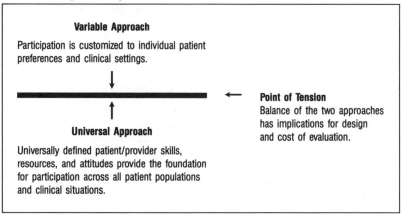

The Basic Model of Participation

In considering the incorporation and evaluation of participation in health care, a reflection on the basic roles of the patient and provider, and the care process and environment should not be overlooked. Figure 3-4 summarizes the interaction between these elements as it occurs in any health care setting. The diagram reinforces that participation has an objective element, based on patients' and providers' available information and skills (such as listening and problem solving), as well as a subjective element that depends on their behaviors and attitudes.

Components of this model are consistent with research regarding the nature of participation.[51] The importance of context (the care environment) is also indicated, recognizing the critical role that setting plays in fostering meaningful participation. An approach to the systematic evaluation of participation can naturally follow, with assessment aimed at the information base, skills, and attitude of patients and providers, and the care processes and structure that create the environment for the interaction.

Key Considerations for Leaders

Based on the discussion in the previous sections, it is obvious that the development of a process to evaluate patient participation is a multifaceted, complex task. To create an effective process, clinical and administrative leaders need to address the following issues at the planning, design, and implementation stages:

- Based on general insights into factors that influence patient preference regarding participation, it is critical that providers routinely elicit information on an individual's preferences. As noted earlier, these expectations can vary dramatically from patient to patient, even when they face identical clinical situations. Additionally, a single patient's preferences can change over time. This predicament suggests that health care organizations and professionals must develop:
  - A routine and efficient capacity for inquiry
  - An effective means of documenting and communicating patient preferences to all providers
  - A process for systematic tracking and analysis of preference trends
- A wealth of complexities and nuances concerning participation have been highlighted in this chapter. Leaders cannot expect to accommodate all of these variables or address all unanswered questions before proceeding. However, they are obligated to acknowledge and understand the variables and design specific care approaches to test various hypotheses concerning the desirability and consequences of participation. By definition, these approaches must include an evaluative component.
- If patient preferences regarding participation are sought, health care systems and delivery processes must be able to accommodate them. This commitment will require investment of resources in staff and patient education; cultivation of increased knowledge regarding clinical conditions, alternative interventions, and outcomes; and, finally, changes in the environment in which care is delivered. For example, if most members of participatory patient populations indicate that they expect discussions to occur in private, an organization's inability to provide an appropriate setting could impair the effectiveness of participation. Beyond that, when

Figure 3-4. Model of the Participatory Process

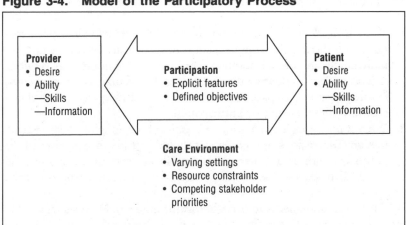

such a gap between expectation and reality occurs in a setting where patient preference was elicited, it could actually provoke dissatisfaction and withdrawal from participation, the very behavior being advocated.

- Care is increasingly fragmented. This condition stems from a combination of factors, including:
  - Structural changes in health care organizations
  - A trend toward specialization in health care
  - Financial constraints that limit contact time in any one component of the health care system
  - Technological advances that make it possible to provide services in alternative settings, such as the home

Consequently, the commitment and capacity necessary to support participation in one setting can be significantly undermined without support and reinforcement from other points along the continuum of care. For instance, consider the care of a pregnant woman. Given the current practices surrounding pregnancy, imagine the challenges — and limited effectiveness — facing a labor and delivery nurse who advocates participation when similar interests did not exist among the obstetricians and office staff with whom the patient interacted before delivery.

Beyond the alignment of provider attitudes, coordination involving the content and timing of conversations and provision of reference materials is clearly required. Considering the various factors that surround participation, it is apparent that increased attention must be provided across a system of care, rather than being isolated within its components.

Conclusion

The evaluation of participation addresses at least three areas:

1. *What is needed?* Evaluating patient requirements regarding participation, with the results being detailed enough that action can be taken — individually and organizationally — by providers of health care services.
2. *Is it occurring?* Evaluating the care processes and practices implemented in direct response to patient preferences and creating greater specificity regarding the meaning of participation.
3. *What is the impact?* Evaluating the results of meaningful patient participation. Dimensions of this analysis should consider perspectives of the patients, health care professionals, and health care organizations, and should also take into account the technical and personal aspects of care.

Such evaluation needs to occur across the industry. However, given that many organizations face more immediate needs, having developed their own agendas in pursuit of this approach to providing care, evaluation must also occur within individual organizations.

With the results of such evaluation in hand, segmentation can take place. Rather than maintaining an oversimplified and inaccurate perspective on participation, additional insights from ongoing study will permit participation to be cultivated and supported for those patients and situations in which it is desired and beneficial—psychologically as well as physiologically. Ironically, retention of a global, "one-size-fits-all" approach undermines the very autonomy that participation is intended to support. M. Gerteis noted that patients "are not always willing—let alone able—to take on such an active role in their own care."[52] Caution is needed to avoid coercion of patients to assume participatory roles they do not desire.[53]

Exercise of autonomy and full participation paradoxically includes the option to choose not to participate, voluntarily transferring responsibility for care and decision making to providers.[54,55] Although this view of patient autonomy may conflict with attitudes regarding the need for individual responsibility that are maintained by some individual providers, it should be considered.

Systematic, credible evaluation will provide the foundation necessary to support participation in a thorough, thoughtful, and individualistic way. The next breakthrough will come when meaningful segmentation of patients is routinely performed, and when health care professionals and organizations are willing and able to respond to the heterogeneous reality surrounding participation in health care.

References

1. Brody, D. S. The patient's role in clinical decision-making. *Annals of Internal Medicine* 93:718–22, 1980.

2. Strull, W. M., Lo, B., and Charles, G. Do patients want to participate in medical decision making? *JAMA* 252(21):2990–94, Dec. 7, 1984.

3. Greenfield, S., Kaplan, S., and Ware, J. E. Expanding patient involvement in care, effects on patient outcomes. *Annals of Internal Medicine* 102:520–28, 1985.

4. Waterworth, S., and Luker, K. A. Reluctant collaborators: do patients want to be involved in decisions concerning care? *Journal of Advanced Nursing* 15:971–76, 1990.

5. Ashworth, P. D., Longmate, M. A., and Morrison, P. Patient participation: its meaning and significance in the context of caring. *Journal of Advanced Nursing* 17:1430–39, 1992.

6. Jewell, S. E. Patient participation: what does it mean to nurses? *Journal of Advanced Nursing* 19:433–38, 1994.

7. Wade, S. Partnership in care: a critical review. *Nursing Standard* 9(48):29–32, Aug. 23, 1995.

8. Katz, J. *The Silent World of Doctor and Patient.* New York City: The Free Press, 1984.

9. World Health Organization. *Formulating Strategies for Health for All for the Year 2000.* Geneva, Switzerland: World Health Organization, 1979, p. 17.

10. Brody, D. S., and others. The relationship between patients' satisfaction with their physicians and perceptions about interventions they desired and received. *Medical Care* 27(11):1027–35, Nov. 1989.

11. Greenfield and others, Expanding patient involvement in care, pp. 525–27.

12. DiMatteo, M. R. Enhancing patient adherence to medical recommendations. *JAMA* 271(1):79,83, Jan. 5, 1994.

13. Macleod-Clark, J., and Latter, S. Working together. *Nursing Times* 86(48):28–31, Nov. 28, 1990.

14. Speedling, E. J., and Rose, D. N. Building an effective doctor–patient relationship: from patient satisfaction to patient participation. *Social Science in Medicine* 21(2):115–20, 1985.

15. Roter, D. L. Patient participation in the patient–provider interaction: the effects of patient question asking on the quality of interaction, satisfaction and compliance. *Health Education Monographs* 5(4):281–315, Winter 1977.

16. Blanchard, C. G., Labrecque, M. S., Ruckdescher, J. C., and Blanchard, E. B. Information and decision-making preferences of hospitalized adult cancer patients. *Social Science in Medicine* 27(11):1139–45, 1988.

17. Deber, R. B. Physicians in health care management 7. The patient–physician partnership: changing roles and the desire for information. *Canadian Medical Association Journal* 151(2):171–76, July 15, 1994.

18. Brody and others, The relationship between patients' satisfaction, p. 719.

19. Strull, Do patient's want to participate . . . ? p. 2993.

20. Ende, J., Kazis, L., Ash, A., and Moskowitz, M. A. Measuring patients' desire for autonomy: decision making and information-seeking preferences among medical patients. *Journal of General Internal Medicine* 4:23–30, Jan./Feb., 1989.

21. Deber, R. B. Physicians in health care management: 8. The patient–physician partnership: decision-making, problem-solving and the desire to participate. *Canadian Medical Association Journal* 151(4):423–27, Aug. 15, 1994.

22. Deber, R. B., Kraetschmer, N., and Irvine, J. What role do patients wish to play in treatment decision making? *Archives of Internal Medicine* 156:1414–20, July 8, 1996.

23. Biley, F. C. Some determinants that effect patient participation in decision-making about nursing care. *Journal of Advanced Nursing* 17:414–21, 1992.

24. Jewell, Patient participation, p. 434.

25. Deber, Physicians in health care management, p. 423.

26. Deber and others, What role do patients wish to play . . . ? p. 1416, 1418.

27. Waterworth and Luker, Reluctant collaborators, p. 974.

28. Ende and others, Measuring patient's desire for autonomy, p. 23.

29. King, B. Techniques for understanding the customer. *Quality Management in Health Care* 2(2):61–67, winter 1994.

30. Tasa, K., Baker, G. R., and Murray, M. Using patient feedback for quality improvement. *Quality Management in Health Care* 4(2):55–67, Winter 1996.

31. Mowery, N., Reavis, P., and Poling, S. R. *Customer Focused Quality*. Knoxville, TN: SPC Press, 1994, chapters 4–6.

32. Dutka, A. *AMA Handbook for Customer Satisfaction: A Complete Guide to Research, Planning and Implementation*. Lincolnwood, IL: NTC Business Books, 1994, chapters 3–5.

33. Ende and others, Measuring patient's desire for autonomy, p. 23.

34. Brody and others, The relationship between patients' satisfaction with their physicians and perceptions about interventions they desired and received, p. 1033.

35. Deber and others, What role do patients wish to play . . . ? pp. 1416, 1418–20.

36. Ovretveit, J. Informed choice? Health service quality and outcome information for patients. *Health Policy* 37:84, 1996.

37. Kasper, J. F., Mulley, A. G., and Wennberg, J. E. Developing shared decision-making programs to improve the quality of health care. *Quality Review Bulletin* 18(6):183–190, June 1992.

38. Randall, T. Producers of videodisc programs strive to expand patient's role in medical decision-making process. *JAMA* 270(2):160, 162, July 14, 1993.

39. Reiley, P., and others. Learning from patients: a discharge planning improvement project. *Journal on Quality Improvement* 22(5):311–22, May 1996.

40. Brody, The patient's role in clinical decision-making, p. 719.

41. Weiss, G. B. Paternalism modernized. *Journal of Medical Ethics* 11:184–87, 1985.

42. Kassirer, J. P. Incorporating patients' preferences into medical decisions. *New England Journal of Medicine* 330(26):1895–96, June 30, 1994.

43. Haug, M. R., and Lavin, B. Practitioner or patient—who's in charge? *Journal of Health and Social Behavior* 22:212–29, Sept. 1981.

44. Deber, Physicians in health care management, p. 424.

45. Biley, Some determinants that effect patient participation, p. 417.

46. Ende and others, Measuring patients' desire for autonomy, p. 27.

47. Ovretveit, Informed choice, pp. 75–90.

48. Strull and others, Do patients want to participate . . . ? p. 2994.

49. Ovretveit, Informed choice, p. 85.

50. Kim, H. S., and others. Patient–nurse collaboration: a comparison of patients' and nurses' attitudes in Finland, Japan, Norway, and the U.S.A. *International Journal of Nursing Studies* 30(5):387–401, 1993.

51. Ashworth and others, Patient participation, pp. 1437–38.

52. Gerteis, M. What patients really want. *Health Management Quarterly* pp. 2–6, third quarter 1993.

53. Waterworth and Luker, Reluctant collaborators, p. 974.

54. Childress, J. F. *Who Should Decide? Paternalism in Health Care.* New York City: Oxford University Press, 1982.

55. Ingelfinger, F. J. Arrogance. *New England Journal of Medicine* 303(26):1507–11, Dec. 25, 1980.

Chapter 4

Partnership in Care

Barbara Balik, RN, MS

Partnerships in care require a commitment to new relationships. Half-hearted attempts at partnering, to see whether it works, will ensure its failure. Partnerships challenge the worldviews of both providers and consumers about their relationship in shaping health care.

Partnerships in health care are nothing new. Long-standing, successful examples of partnerships exist in some community health, pediatric, oncology, and birthing settings. The need for and interest in partnerships in all health care settings are accelerating. This chapter provides a framework to help partners structure their roles, identify necessary behaviors, and identify the elements for advancing partnerships to achieve improved health within the community.

The chapter also offers suggestions to nursing leaders on how to begin or to accelerate partnerships in care. Identifying the steps necessary to create partnerships enhances the health care experience and outcomes for patients and their families.*

Navigating the transitions from current provider–patient relationships to meaningful partnerships requires a complex combination of changes for individual caregivers, shifts in consumer expectations and behaviors, and changes in organizational culture. Though the process is not short term or linear, there are key areas on which nursing leaders can focus and ways in which they can leverage their efforts toward achieving partnerships. The key navigational points include:

- Defining a framework
- Conducting a reality assessment
- Ensuring integration
- Nurturing exemplars and champions

---

*All references to "patient" in this chapter are understood to include both the patient and his or her family.

- Seeking out and celebrating stories
- Pushing the margins
- Negotiating the changes
- Building the toolbox
- Advancing the partnership

This chapter addresses each of these key points in detail.

Defining a Partnership Framework

Nurse executives first need to clarify the framework needed to describe the partnership. This clarification must be done collaboratively with patients and providers. The first step is for providers to examine how they involve patients in the care experience and then how they think patients perceive this relationship. A successful framework addresses the following questions:

- *What is the partnership?* The provider needs to ask, "In my interactions with patients and families, how do I see my relationship with them?" Providers who are sincerely interested in partnerships may answer that they are committed to an open exchange of information, that they recognize the strengths and skills the patient brings to the interaction, that there is a need to listen more than tell, and that the patient is capable of directing his or her care in collaboration with the provider.
- *What does the partnership look like in action?* In this case, the provider should ask, "If I believe in partnerships, what will I or others see happen in my interactions with patients and families?" The answers to this question may vary, but some aspects may include the incorporation of patient information and patient choices in care plan development and delivery, the empowerment of the patient to direct key aspects of care according to what he or she views as therapeutic, the respect of patient timetables and the use of the timetables to create care schedules, and the incorporation of negotiation as a constant aspect of care delivery to reflect the provider's knowledge and skills as well as those of the patient.
- *What are the outcomes?* At this point, the provider should address the questions: "Are my goals and progress measures for patients the same as theirs? Do we speak the same language in describing expected outcomes?" Some providers may find that they stymie patients' ability to participate by giving more importance and credence to provider-defined outcomes than to patient wishes or by using unexplained technical language in discussing conditions and treatments. When both partners use similar language, it reinforces the effective communication required to meet partnership goals and accelerate the healing process.

- *Is the partnership based on the consumer's voice or does it solely reflect the providers' view?* Here, the provider needs to determine, "Do the patient and I share common goals?" Under the concept of partnership, the patient's voice is heard in all stages of care, including planning and delivery. Patients should be able to describe aspects of their plans of care, the course of their care, and expected outcomes.
- *Does the partnership clearly describe a desired future state?* In assessing this point, the provider asks, "Do I share my patients' long-term views of their care?" Whether a patient is in an acute care setting where the future state may be described in goals for the next 12 hours or in an ambulatory setting where care may proceed for months, he or she needs to work with the provider toward a shared (usually negotiated) goal.

Once they have addressed these questions from their own point of view, providers need to verify their own perceptions by asking patients the same questions. The language used in approaching these issues should be tailored to the patient's strengths, skills, and needs. The gathering of all necessary information on these points cannot be achieved in one encounter but requires ongoing conversations.

Conducting a Reality Assessment

Nurse executives need to make an honest assessment of their institution's current reality. In our current reality, health care settings are primarily provider centered. Health care providers articulate and defend their patient-centered views, but an analysis of their systems, structures, and language illustrates the gap between stated values and values in action. Although leaders can describe specific instances of this gap, the most illustrative tool is the patient's own voice. An example is the work of the quality council in the surgical center at United Hospital in St. Paul, MN. The council is composed of multidisciplinary clinical and support staff and administrative leaders. They regularly analyze the results of the patient satisfaction survey to identify opportunities for improvement in postoperative care.

The council was stymied by their lack of progress in some patient satisfaction areas and recognized that their reporting methods may have been limiting their improvement efforts. Many surveys do not provide a sufficient level of detail to identify opportunities and direct resolution. They lack the specific topic areas for addressing patient care concerns. The council, in pursuit of more robust information to improve care, partnered with an internal resource—a planning and communications staff member with expertise in conducting focus groups—to conduct patient focus groups stratified by gender and age. The qualitative data in the verbatim transcripts of patient stories provided the team with additional information that was actionable by the staff in improving care. The stories contained a wealth of meaningful information.

The quality council heard stories from the patients' perspective, unfiltered by provider interpretation. Content analysis of the transcriptions identified themes in the experience of women who had undergone elective surgery and men with a diagnosis of cancer being treated surgically. The themes indicated that women, in general, had higher expectations for promptness in responding to call signals, pain medication, and nurse response time, as well as higher expectations about cleanliness and food quality. Male patients recognized broader time frames for response time and pain management, and were more likely to voice appreciation for their care. It was also found that types of surgery may influence patient responses, since the women studied had elective surgery, whereas the men underwent diagnostic or therapeutic cancer surgery. These data informed the council of opportunities for improvement by providing population-specific information rather than data from the general experience of all patients. As a result, the surgical staff partnered with colleagues in United's Birth Center to learn more about developing and providing "woman-friendly" services.

Another means of assessing current reality is to analyze the values we espouse and those we reflect by our actions. Are they congruent, or is there a gap? Observing values in action is a method to determine how we actually behave rather than how we say we behave. In this kind of assessment, provider groups and administrative leaders identify the values they hold regarding partnerships with patients and involvement in patient-centered systems. They become detectives in their environment, observing behavior through the eyes of patients to determine whether behavior, systems, and experiences at the point of service reflect or are in conflict with stated values. Assigning providers to conduct this analysis during their work time results in insights that lead to positive changes. Areas of observation and assessment include:

- *Language used:* What terms, initials, or jargon are used? Is the same language used with patients, health care providers, and nonclinical staff? Who uses a title? Who does not?
- *Use of time:* Who waits for whom? Is it usually the provider who determines when activities occur?
- *Rules:* What are the rules for how things get done, and who makes the rules?

Ensuring Integration

The framework for partnerships in care needs to be linked with strategy, key systems, and core values. Failure to link partnerships results in efforts in which partnership is approached as a project or initiative rather than a core philosophy. Areas in which partnership can be integrated include:

- Organizational values
- Key organizational strategies
- Quality philosophy and measurement
- Patient care delivery models

Health care systems need to identify their values. (See figure 4-1 for an example for Allina.) The values guide how the organization will behave as it executes the strategies to fulfill its vision and its mission, which is to provide an excellent health care experience for customers. With these values, we can observe whether our decisions and practices reflect the values of service and partnership with our patients, and we can hold each other accountable for actions that embody those values.

Figure 4-1.   Allina Values

Service
- Providing compassionate care
- Treating individuals with dignity and respect
- Delivering excellence in all our services and products
- Placing the needs of those we serve above our own

Innovation
- Learning continuously
- Embracing and implementing change
- Experimenting, testing, and exploring new possibilities
- Anticipating tomorrow's needs today

Partnership
- Honoring commitments
- Recognizing and strengthening interdependencies
- Capturing the benefits of differing points of view
- Supporting collective obligations

Stewardship
- Using our resources wisely
- Demonstrating financial accountability
- Making decisions on behalf of the future
- Earning community trust

Integrity
- Telling the truth
- Matching our actions with our words
- Building a reputation of reliability and constancy
- Using these values as a collective guide for our actions

©Allina Health System 1996

Grounded in commonly held values, the key organizational strategies can set the direction for developing partnerships. Strategies that reflect short-term thinking and limit providers' commitment to partnerships clearly convey the message that the organization is not interested in the patient's role in care. Some strategies that support partnerships are establishing goals related to understanding patients' strengths and skills, and incorporating patients' stated needs and expectations in program development and ongoing assessment. United Hospital uses a patient/family advisory council to seek advice and direction regarding redesign activities, patient education materials and processes, and a variety of care and service topics.

Finally, patient care delivery models that focus on provider accountability also support partnerships. Rates for cesarean births, calculated individually for each nurse, are shared in United's Birth Center to assist nurses in assessing their ability to partner with childbearing families in achieving a low-intervention birth experience.

Nurturing Exemplars and Champions

Developing partnerships in care requires concrete examples for others to emulate. Providers learn from those they consider to be role models or mentors and by observing positive patient outcomes and patient appreciation of care. One means of advancing partnership is to identify exemplary practice and to convey its importance to others. In health care organizations with few partnerships, the exemplars are often voices from the fringe with persistent and isolated messages. They probably have promoted methods that colleagues see as radical, time consuming, or unnecessary. Occasionally, colleagues may accuse them of undermining safe patient care.

Leaders or providers who experienced the changes in birthing practices in the early 1970s are familiar with exemplars and champions. Consumers and some health care champions advocated greater choice and voice for families in the birthing process, less invasive treatment, and active presence and participation by fathers. Those in opposition described the champions as unprofessional and saw including fathers in delivery rooms as an unsafe practice. Those early efforts have now become the standards of care.

One champion, a critical care manager, has worked tirelessly in her hospital to create a family-centered intensive care unit (ICU). Using a local pediatric hospital as a model, she first eliminated visiting restrictions. Convincing nurses to abandon the "one person, 10 minutes every hour" rule was a long process. The manager helped staff evolve from making rule-based decisions to making assessment-based decisions regarding visiting and family participation. Nurses needed to learn to assess which stimuli hindered patient progress and which contributed to healing. The family came to be seen as a support and aid to healing. This champion recognized that partnership is impossible if one partner, in this case, the family, is absent. The manager also identified a constellation of champions within the department that allowed staff to develop a supportive network of partnerships.

Seeking Out and Celebrating Stories

In most organizations, partnerships require cultural changes. Stories are an effective tool to describe change and its results and benefits. Leaders who seek out and ask for these stories can propel cultural transformation or modification. Leaders convey values and "how we do things" through the stories they tell. A nurse executive shares the celebration story of critical care nurses who were debating which sleeping cot for a family member folded up fastest. The nurses had moved from the perspective of "Family members do not sleep in ICU rooms" to "How do we best meet both the needs of family presence and emergency response?" The debate about the functionality of cots represented a change toward embracing family partnerships in care. Small steps in advancing the partnership show the way for others. Stories shared verbally or in official communications need to describe the small steps and emphasize their positive impact.

Pushing the Margins

Small steps are essential, but it is also necessary to "push the margins," or occasionally take some bold, aggressive (and well-thought-out) steps. The satisfaction of completing small steps can lull providers and leaders into complacency about how well they are doing. Consumers are intolerant of continual small steps.

Pediatric settings can often show other health care providers how far they still have to go. Leading pediatric centers exemplify family-centered care as a model of partnership. For example, a hospital may decide to buddy nurses from an adult ICU with nurses from a pediatric ICU and challenge those from the adult facility to identify all the restrictions present in their unit but absent in the pediatric setting. The "push" is to ask why the adult setting is so restrictive and how quickly they can break down the old barriers. Models can then be used to design and revise the ICU delivery system.

Leaders need to develop some healthy tension between their organization's current activities and the desired future state. Providing examples of advanced partnerships, such as those in the pediatric setting, is one way to create healthy tension. The family-centered care model outlined in figure 4-2 reflects the changes needed, particularly on the part of providers, to develop partnerships.[1] The elements are incorporated into policy and practice in all areas of service and care. They become the guiding principles for

Figure 4-2.   Key Elements of Family-Centered Care

- The individual family is the constant, while the service system and personnel within those systems fluctuate.
- Individual/family and professional collaboration is facilitated across the continuum of services, in the development, implementation, and evaluation of programs, and in policy development.
- There is a complete and unbiased exchange of information between the individual/family and professionals in a supportive manner in all interactions.
- The diversity within and across each family is recognized and respected. Decisions about care are accomplished through collaborative interactions, not by predetermining the individual or family's needs or strengths, or making assumptions based on their culture, ethnicity, religious beliefs, education, or other qualities.
- Different methods of coping are recognized and respected.
- Services and systems are flexible, accessible, and comprehensive to meet individual/family identified needs.
- Families are appreciated as families and individuals, recognizing that they possess a wide range of strengths, concerns, emotions, and aspirations beyond their health care needs.

the development of partnership, the acquisition of needed skills, and the reconfiguration of relationships.

To appreciate the relationship changes needed, a description of models of service delivery is offered that reflects a continuum of interactions between consumers and providers. This framework has demonstrated success in a variety of pediatric settings and is transferable to other health care institutions and systems. The framework recognizes that the partners in health care interactions are people in a family within the context of a community rather than isolated, autonomous islands. Listening to and understanding how the family defines itself is the basis for family-centered care. This framework describes the worldview required to transform health care relationships and delivery.

The four models of service delivery include professionally centered, family allied, family focused, and family centered.[2] They reflect a range from the current, common state (professionally centered) to an idealized vision or state (family centered). Some organizations have progressed significantly toward the family-centered environment, although most can consider themselves somewhere on the path to this goal. A range of models may be present within one organization at any time as different groups of providers change and grow. It is fair to call this a developmental model, though all organizations will not go through each stage. It would not be surprising for a provider group making a transition from the family-allied to the family-centered stage to skip the family-focused stage.

Professionally Centered or System-Centered Models

In this model, providers offer help so those in need can function in a less dysfunctional, less ill manner. The providers plan and implement the interventions, and families are viewed as lacking the skills necessary to solve their problems. The delivery of service is driven by the needs identified by the institution.

Family-Allied Models

At this stage, consumers have an active role in the care and services they receive but are treated as agents of the providers. As implementers of the services or interventions, patients and families have a minimal role in the articulation of choices, design, location, timing, or evaluation of services.

Family-Focused Models

At this point, collaboration increases with more of a consumer orientation toward families, but the family is still dependent on providers for advice and guidance. Provider networks of services are emphasized over community or family networks.

Family-Centered Models

In this model, patients and families are not just consumers of services but dictate practices. Their needs and decisions determine aspects of service delivery. Providers are agents and instruments of consumers and intervene in ways that promote patient/family decision making, capabilities, and competencies. This model relies on the true partnership: Patients, families, and providers are of mutual benefit as integral members of a team in which members share information from their unique perspectives. Networks are developed that tap into family and community resources that continue after health care services end.

Negotiating the Changes

Negotiating the changes from provider-centered to partnership or family-centered models requires:

- A recognition that partnerships are complex.
- Development of skills in providers who may not want to relinquish their sense of control and patients/families who are unsure of this new role. Such skills include the ability to positively address conflict, the ability to reflect on current practice and partnerships and learn from experience, a recognition that caring includes incorporation of patient skills and strengths, and the ability to address one's own power issues as partnerships challenge old boundaries of control in care.
- The development of communication skills, especially active listening, by all providers.

- Identification of the knowledge required for a patient to participate in decision making. We must not initially expect consumers to think of all implications, alternatives, or questions.
- Use of a common language without jargon and distancing terminology that emphasizes the gap between providers and patients.
- Patience with the discomfort of consumers who seek "the one answer."
- The development of relationships over time.
- An acceptance of the short-term costs of conversations between patients and providers that are required to offset the long-term savings of improved decision making and use of resources.

The development of partnerships initially means there needs to be reflection on the world view (age, cultural background, gender, spiritual beliefs, and so on) that the provider brings to the interaction. The intent to plan together to achieve a health outcome cannot be contingent on how well the consumer fits a definition of partnership created by the provider alone. Partnerships will vary by individual and family. The partnership skills will develop over time as those involved gain more knowledge of each other and what each contributes, and as the needs or gains are identified. Use of an asset-based rather than deficit-based perspective helps the provider see the strengths, no matter how limited they initially appear.

An example is the view a provider holds of an ill, 70-year-old woman. Does the provider see a frail, debilitated, dependent patient who may not seek information or participate in her care decision? Or does the provider see a frail patient who brings a life history as a strong matriarch, beloved mother and grandmother, the unusual college graduate for her era, and business manager for the family business?[3] The knowledge of consumers and the view of their capabilities influence providers' interactions and, often, health care interactions. A department's or an organization's assessment of where on the continuum from provider-centered to family-centered it falls can also be part of the second navigational point, an honest assessment.

Building the Toolbox

Working with stakeholders, leaders must develop the systems and structures to provide enabling systems for caring partnerships to emerge. Different learning styles — including varying reading levels, visual or written preference, and so on — must be considered in planning these systems. The key is to find out from patients how they like to learn; for example, asking how they like to tackle a new project or task at home.

Building a partnership requires concrete tools. The Association for the Care of Children's Health offers materials such as checklists to assess systems and interactions in family-centered care. These can be generalized to a variety of settings.[4] (See figure 4-3.)

Figure 4-3.   How Information Is Exchanged: A Checklist

- Attention is paid to body language. Is your hand on the door knob as you ask questions? Location and events surrounding communication say as much as the actual information provided.
- Excellent listening skills are used.
- Information is up to date, complete, unbiased, and comes from multiple sources including other consumers.
- Common courtesy is exhibited: returning phone calls, acknowledging written correspondence, listening to people, treating people with respect.
- Open-ended questions are asked:
  —How are things going?
  —Has anything different or unusual happened to you or your family since our last visit?
  —Is there anything else you need to know?
  —Is there anything else we need to know?
  —Do you have all the information you want about your clinical status, test results, treatment options?
  —Do you have all the information you want about community resources?
  —Do you have the information you need to manage on your own?
  —What needs to be changed?
  —What needs to stay the same?
  —Who or what is helpful?

For example, consumer knowledge is a foundation for building a partnership. The exchange of complete and unbiased information requires that an assessment be undertaken to determine if there is bias, how to identify it, and what modes of transmission are available to meet different consumer learning needs. In most settings, providers offer extensive information. Several key questions need to be asked about this information before it is shared with patients:

- Is it the essential content for a basic understanding of the topic?
- Is it in understandable form—reading level, jargon?
- Is it in a variety of formats—words, pictures, tapes?
- Can patients review it at their own speed?
- Can it be added to as the patient gains knowledge and has more questions?

Rather than adding more content, this area calls for understanding information needs from the patient's perspective. All consumer information does not have to change at once. The focus is on improving the efficiency and effectiveness of information transfer based on well-established adult learning principles.

Advancing the Partnership

Partnerships can advance in systems of care between individual providers and patients and when philosophy of partnership permeates all aspects of the system. Individual providers are the crucial interface between health networks and consumers. Systems of care with embedded partnership behaviors support the individual providers and avoid the need to reestablish partnership principles at every encounter.

Patients who expect partnership behavior from all providers and find that systems reinforce those behaviors will more consistently interact with all providers as partners. Patients who learn that asking questions, being an equal member of the team, and speaking up are expected and encouraged will be more confident partners. They also become better at self-care and consume fewer health care resources because they make better decisions and frequently choose less invasive, more conservative approaches. They use emergency departments less often because they have a better knowledge about the health care system and can use it more productively. On the other hand, patients who discover that some providers are threatened will be limited in their involvement, which in turn limits the ability for joint planning and improved outcomes.

The consistency of providers and systems about partnerships also addresses concerns around time. Initially, creating partnership takes more time. Asking rather than telling, answering questions, discussing options, and seeking clarification adds to interaction time. Partnership is the commitment to establish long-term, empowered relationships, with the belief that consumers will influence changes in the health care system to benefit themselves and the entire community. Providers can initiate partnerships in any encounter and in any setting. The spirit and intent of partnerships begin in the essential interaction between the provider and the individual/family.

References

1. Shelton, T., and Smith-Stepanek, J. *Family-Centered Care for Children Needing Specialized Health and Developmental Services*. Bethesda, MD: Association for the Care of Children's Health, with support from the Maternal and Child Health Bureau, U.S. Department of Health and Human Services, 1994, p. vii.

2. Shelton and Smith-Stepanek, *Family-Centered Care*, p. 6.

3. Lyn Ceronsky, clinical nurse specialist and coordinator, Center for Breast Care, United Hospital, St. Paul. Personal communication, Jan. 1997.

4. Association for the Care of Children's Health, Bethesda, MD.

Partnership: The Milestone for Quality and Service

Julianne M. Morath, RN, MS

"The patient is not an actuarial table. She's your mother." This aphorism by J. D. Beckham epitomizes the perspective necessary to effect patient participation within the organizational context.[1] For health care to truly improve health, the patient must become part of the system, not merely have input into the system.

As preceding chapters have described, this simple notion requires complex cultural changes in attitudes, processes, and overall systems. It means that the provider and care team create the health care experience in partnership with an informed patient. The creation of an enduring health care experience aimed at improving the health status of the patient through partnership is the subject of this book. This chapter focuses on the process necessary to create an environment in which partnerships can develop and become an established part of the health care system.

The Call to Action

Among the most exciting changes in health care today is the questioning of traditional care boundaries and the provider–patient relationship structures that have emerged largely through an industrywide focus on quality. Historically, care has been provided by experts in clinics, hospitals, and medical centers. It was directed solely toward healing or improving the patient's physical condition rather than providing informed choices, increasing participation, or encouraging independence.

In the groundbreaking *Through the Patient's Eyes*, Gerteis exploded the myth of "doctor or clinician knows best." Eclipsing the often self-serving satisfaction surveys used to gauge the quality of care provided, Gerteis studied and learned from patients themselves what mattered. Repeatedly, she found that information, choice, participation, coordination of transitions, and knowing that preferences would be respected and honored were the critical measures of satisfaction for patients.[2]

These critical measures underscore the idea that patients are asking to become part of the health system, not passive recipients of its services. The Picker Institute organized Gerteis' findings into seven dimensions of care that can be measured, studied, and improved. (See table 5-1.) These dimensions, which concern patients, also require providers' attention if true partnerships are to emerge. The clinician and patient must be able to appreciate each other's concerns, perspectives, skills, and contributions before they can enter the health care experience as partners.

Why should an organization consider transforming its health care processes to fully involve the patient? First, it is the right and ethical thing to do. It also makes good business sense. Multiple studies and sources tell us that it is the experience of care the patient values. It is the experience of care that creates loyalty. It is the experience of care over time that provides the opportunities to improve health status. And it is the experience of care that builds market share. The findings of one integrated health care system that analyzed the results from focus groups, satisfaction surveys, and consumer interviews and studies describe the care experience desired by patients and members in their own words. (See figure 5-1.)

This assertion is often startling to clinicians who have dedicated their professional careers to providing clinical quality in their practices. To say that the experience of care is the distinguishing factor in determining quality in the patient's eyes is not to supplant clinical quality. Quite the contrary—clinical quality is an assumed foundation of the care experience.

There is a greeting in South Africa, described by Lawrence Vander Post, that translates as "I see you."[3] It implies that to be a person means to be acknowledged as an individual and be in relationships with others. Isn't this

Table 5-1. Dimensions of Care

For Inpatients	For Clinic Patients
Respect for patient preferences	Respect for patient preferences
Coordination of care	Access
Information and education	Information and education
Physical comfort	
Emotional support	Emotional support
Involvement of family and friends	
Continuity and transition	Continuity and coordination

Source: ©The Picker Institute, Boston, MA, 1995.

Figure 5-1. Patient Requirements for a Positive Experience of Care

> - "I get what I need when I need it, easily."
> - "I am a knowledgeable partner in my health care."
> - "I am pleasantly surprised by my experience."
> - "I believe Allina and its staff are competent."
> - "I am respected as an individual and treated with dignity."
> - "I feel safe and secure."

Source: Floyd, M., Morath, J., and others, Service Excellence Team, Allina Health System, 1996.

what patients are saying to providers? "See me—not my diagnosis; my risk; my expected cost per hospital day, DRG, or PMPM—but who I am. What I think, fear, need, and prefer."

Clinicians must move from the expert role in which they are the ones giving others information to a role in which they listen and learn from others. This new role requires partnership skills, aligned incentives, and an environment that supports it. For example, clinics that work on a production model requiring a maximum of 15 minutes per patient visit present a challenge. In this setting, a physician ordered an ultrasound for an anxious pregnant mother to reassure her that her baby was fine. The physician explained the rationale for the cost of the technology as follows: The use of ultrasonography was reimbursable; the extra time it would take to understand the young woman's apprehension was not. An opportunity for a partnership between the physician and patient was missed.

As the clinician–patient partnership is explored, clinicians bear the responsibility of being knowledgeable, current, technically proficient, and skilled in integrating aspects of care. Patients are responsible for entering the partnership as full participants in learning about their health, advocating their preferences, exploring options, and reducing their health risks.

How to Get Started

For partnership to become a cornerstone for improvement, it requires more than clinicians' good intentions and patients' desire to assume greater responsibility for their health and health care decisions. An organizational context or framework needs to be developed in which partnering with patients and families is expected, measured, and rewarded. Bringing the patient into the care system as a full participant must become a normal part of how the organization or system does its work rather than an optional exercise. The processes of providing care and designing support systems must be based on a knowledge of the customer's (patient's) requirements and preferences.

Even if a clinician or system cannot meet patient expectations in a particular situation, those expectations must be acknowledged and dealt with openly.

In partnership, missed expectations or disagreements provide opportunities for improvement, a chance to discover new options. This area is uncomfortable and uncertain for many providers, as experience is limited. Partnership means entering into value-based decision making and practice in which values are explicitly defined. A broader definition of diversity is required as clinicians attempt to find creative new ways to honor these values. New attitudes, new behaviors, and organizational ethics need to come together in an environment that supports such changes.

Although these challenges may seem daunting, most health care organizations, providers, and consumers have begun the journey toward partnership. The following briefly describes the progression of such a journey, from a traditional expert model to a total quality model:

1. *Status quo expert model:* In this traditional model, health care is provided from the "clinician-knows-best" standpoint and the patient is a passive recipient. Communication is a one-way encounter.
2. *Patient (customer) service model:* This model recognizes that problems arise in the provision of care—for example, failures in processes or products. Many organizations respond to these problems by appointing patient representatives, through whom providers receive feedback from patients. Anecdotal accounts of patient problems are used as a basis for correcting problems. This is the first step toward two-way communication.
3. *Quality control model:* Quality control evolves as a reaction to accumulated patient complaints. Commonly referred to as "quality assurance," this model assumes that people are the cause of problems. Standards are set, individual performance is measured, and practitioners who do not meet standard performance levels are punished. Often, standards are narrowed, and higher levels of performance are expected. This environment inhibits two-way communication: Patient feedback is not desired because providers are less likely to explore alternative care options for fear of reprisal.
4. *Continuous quality improvement model:* At this level of evolution, the focus of improvement efforts shifts to processes instead of people. Patient requirements are used as input in establishing processes and measuring and evaluating quality. The communication at this stage is usually internally focused on specific unit or departmental processes rather than on organizational systems as a whole.
5. *Total quality model:* At the highest level of quality evolution, total quality involves partnership and systemwide solicitation of information. Organization leaders establish a vision which is used to attract and inspire commitment and loyalty. The distinguishing feature of this model is that

it focuses on bringing the patient, family, and community into the system rather than delivering a service to them. Patient participation and preferences are used to create value-based services and products, and enduring partnerships are valued and nurtured. Communication is open and encouraged between all partners (the organization, patients and families, the community, third-party payers, managed care corporations, and so on). (See figure 5-2.)

Once an organization has reached the total quality stage, knowledge about patients is acquired through a variety of sources and is applied in all aspects of business. Sources include focus groups, consumer-affairs panels, consumer and community boards and committees, and product design structures in which customers are actively involved. A respectful and therapeutic environment is evident in which patients have access to information and resources and are informed partners with clinicians and the care team in planning for their health. An organization of this type embodies value-based practices and decision making. Shared values among patients, community, and organizations are developed to guide practice, support decision making, and help identify areas of potential conflict for which resolution processes are developed. Value-based decision making and practice form the ethics of the organization.[4]

When an organization has reached the total quality stage, it has created an environment for meaningful conversations between partners and the development of shared visions and values. Partners dealings with each other are based on mutual respect, honesty, courage, and humility. This environment is exceptional; and doesn't it make sense that health care should lead the way in developing such an environment?

Figure 5-2. The Total Quality Model

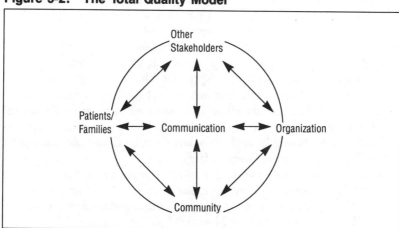

If health care is to be redefined to deal with today's challenges (see the epilogue to this book), it needs to start with a "journey from within" for those who have the ability and responsibility to provide leadership—namely, clinicians. Each provider needs to address the following questions:

- What leadership model do I follow? What model does my organization follow?
- How do I approach learning about patients' preferences and new care alternatives?
- How do I partner with administrative colleagues, clinicians, and other staff members?
- Do I ask questions about others' opinions and consider their answers?
- Do I identify and understand patients' and families' requirements?
- Do I model the changes I hope to see in the health care environment?

These questions form a basis for addressing the steps to achieving a total quality environment discussed in the following sections.

Assessing the Existing Environment

The nurse executive is a key leader in enabling an organization to move along its quality journey and learn to partner with the customer. In doing so, nurse executives must ask themselves some assessment questions:

- *What are my current sources of information about patients?* For example, do I have a patient satisfaction survey system and complaint system? Do I conduct or attend patient/family focus groups? Do I keep a journal of qualitative information I receive from patients and families when making rounds? Do I have community- or constituency-based listening posts in the community at large? Do I have a way for staff to tell me about their experiences with patients and families?
- *How do I disseminate and use that information?* For example, do I routinely talk about customer requirements in staff meetings? Do I have mechanisms to report survey findings? Do I have local (unit-based) mirrors of hospital or system measurements about patient satisfaction or requirements that are relevant to and can be acted on at the front line? Are educational offerings and curricula built around customer requirements and feedback? How do I convert process failures and complaints into learning or improvement opportunities?
- *What do I ask about, measure, and monitor as a reflection of what I value?* For example, Do my questions focus on budget and workload, or do they address understanding whether care and services are improving? What do I ask about first? How do I phrase my inquiry? Do I recognize the current clinical reality of my setting?

- *How do I spend my time, and how do I stay close to the customer?* For example, have I arranged my schedule according to what is meaningful and valuable to me? Do I consciously make time to spend time with my customers?
- *What systems do I have in place to ensure that customers' voices are heard in my decision making?* For example, do I regularly have quantitative and qualitative data available to support decision making? Are the data systematically acquired and analyzed over time to evaluate the results of decision making?
- *What performance and outcome feedback is available to clinicians that is relevant and can be acted upon at the front line?* For example, are there performance profiles focusing on key process and outcome measures to be achieved? Are interdisciplinary teams provided with regular feedback on the results of their efforts, including communication with patients, informing patients, respecting preferences, and encouraging joint planning of care?
- *Are measurement and feedback used for learning and improvement?* For example, how do I address staff mistakes, patient complaints, and process failures? Are these events seen as opportunities for learning and improvement? Do I look for improvement over time and across departmental boundaries? Do staff members only hear from me when performance is declining? Do I celebrate learning and improvement? Do I improve my own performance through feedback mechanisms? Is my leadership team improving its methods?
- *What are my vehicles and strategies for compiling or disseminating patient information?* For example, do I optimize educational and publishing resources as strategic methods of disseminating and reinforcing partnering strategies? Do I know who practice exemplars are? Do I have mechanisms to tell their stories to staff members? Do consumers participate in meetings or quality improvement teams? Do I have access to and knowledge of how to use technology such as Intranet, public service announcements, and interactive video? Do patient education strategies reflect patient needs and preferences? Were they created with patients and/or community members? Are translation services or multilingual materials available in visual, auditory, and even kinesthetic presentations? Most important, what investment have I made in developing the clinical staff's skills in listening and consulting and in incorporating patient requirements and preferences in collaborative care decisions and wellness/prevention strategies? What percentage of the salary budget is used for education?

Assessing Patient Needs and Expectations

Research emphasizes the necessity of including patients' expectations and enlisting their participation in the care process. There is evidence that doing so improves both the physiological and the satisfaction outcomes of care. Partnering with the patient is not merely a response to customer demands; it can improve health. J. C. Hornberger, H. Habraken, and D. Bloch concluded that patients desire more involvement than ever in decisions affecting their health; and patients who are integral partners in health care decisions are more satisfied with care, adhere more readily to recommendations, and experience better health outcomes.[5]

In his examination of research on patient satisfaction and the factors that influence attitudes in primary care, J. Rees Lewis noted that quality of care is frequently assessed by provider- or government-derived measures rather than by dimensions patients themselves consider important.[6] His work challenges organizations around "modified paternalism" or "tokenism." For Lewis, listening is a sign of respect and caring. The provider who fails to listen may miss the real concern of the patient and the opportunity to provide care. Patients miss the opportunity to be an involved participant in their care and the experience of being cared for.[7]

Research continues to address the issue of what patients want in the area of participation. In her studies of patient partnerships, Raisa Deber makes the distinction that wanting to know is not the same as being in charge.[8] Until that distinction is explored and understood, the roles of patient and provider will not be clear, and genuine shared decision making will not be possible. She explores the continuum from sensitive paternalism to informed consent and concludes that neither results in shared decision making. To achieve this goal, she suggests that patients and providers need to clearly focus on the following care topics and explore each fully:

- Available alternatives
- Potential outcomes of each alternative
- Costs, risks, and benefits of each alternative
- Values of each potential outcome

Mutual understanding of and satisfactory agreement on each topic moves the provider–patient relationship to a partnership based on the content of care decisions.

Integrating Partnership and Cost Control

Many nurse executives are now working with health plans or in integrated health care systems that include financing mechanisms and care management. For them, "demand management" is a term that is gaining significance. The premise of demand management is that health care utilization and costs will be reduced significantly only when the demand for health care services from the consumer is reduced.[9]

Demand management again raises the issue of patient access to information, counseling, and partnership. It uses decision making and self-management support systems to enable and encourage consumers to make appropriate use of health care resources. It is rational and information based. There is evidence that individuals with access to self-help and self-care have greater confidence in their ability to self-manage and less dependence on health care providers. Individuals who consciously choose healthy lifestyles tend to need less medical care for preventable illnesses.[10] They also are able to exercise informed choice and choose less risky options that tend to be less costly.[11]

Of course, individuals do not always spontaneously choose healthy lifestyles. Nurse executives are required to design and implement enabling systems, such as the following:

- Nurse-staffed phone lines for information, counseling, and consultations.
- Psychosocial support for patients and families who face difficult decisions, including opportunities to rehearse possible scenarios before decisions are necessary, particularly in the area of palliative care and medical futility.
- Organized systems (such as a health counselor or a case management system) to assist individuals in managing chronic disease. These systems might include a day planner with relevant information, medication schedules, physician appointments, logs for self-monitoring physiological parameters (such as glucose level), treatment and/or activity regimes, and a journal for keeping track of questions to ask the clinician or suggestions from the clinician. Using the planner, the patient manages and owns his or her care plan.
- Health promotion programs and products, including individual risk assessments and immediate feedback on behavior changes to enhance wellness; partnering with health clubs, schools, and community groups for health education and fitness activities; and dissemination of age-specific U.S. Health Prevention Guidelines, such as environmental risk assessments for infants and toddlers.

Obtaining Clinician Buy-In

Given the evidence of need for patient partnerships, clinicians still face barriers to thinking about patients as informed partners in care. The following contentions that an informed patient interferes with the physician–patient relationship must be addressed:[12]

1. Patients should be passive and essentially be nonparticipants in decision making and management of their health and medical problems.
2. Physicians should be the source of all health and medical information.

3. Services that diagnose, prescribe, or offer second opinions raise quality-of-care questions.

Whereas points 1 and 2 have been explored throughout this chapter, point 3 requires some discussion. There is a long-standing belief that all providers have the same knowledge of medical science and that medical science is certain. This belief has little tolerance for uncertainty, and differences in opinion often give rise to doubt and concern about provider competency. This is a quality issue. The ability to take in, discuss, and weigh a differing second opinion can provide the opportunity for a broader consideration of alternatives and options. It requires greater personal responsibility on the patient's side to participate in these dilemmas and a willingness on the provider's side to consider and explore alternatives to his or her standard outlook.

When faced with a variety of options, the patient needs support in care decisions. Current systems are not well prepared to offer this kind of support. However, with increasing frequency, patients arrive at provider appointments armed with the latest guidelines, protocols, and published articles; information available on the Internet; and advice from friends and relatives who have shared similar health experiences. As medical knowledge becomes more readily available, both patients and providers will gain experience at working together to explore differing opinions, to consider preferences and options, and, in the many instances in which medical evidence is inconclusive, to use patient preference as a basis for treatment and care-planning decisions.

Tools for Preparing the Patient

In addition to the blizzard of consumer-oriented health promotion and health care literature available, tools such as broad Internet search capabilities, provider-specific and health system–specific home pages on the World Wide Web, and interactive CD-ROM software provide patients and other consumers with access to health and medical information. Programs for specific condition information and monitoring are available in various languages. Most health care organizations have increased their community education initiatives to include telemedicine and television broadcasts. Also, more and more organizations require or use process and outcome measures to inform the public about general health care, the organization itself, and, in some instances, provider- and group-specific performance.

A looming issue rests in the question of how an informed consumer will act in making health care choices. This leads to the idea of creating tools such as report cards that patients can use when selecting physicians, health plans, and hospitals. The theory is that when patients (employers or public buyers of health care) have comparative information about the outcomes, costs, and satisfaction associated with different providers, health plans, and delivery systems, they will choose the options that excel. Competition will do the rest to improve quality and hold down costs.[13] Although issues of technological capability, safeguarding privacy of patient data, and questions of how data would be released to providers have modified initial plans, this area continues to warrant the attention of nurses.

Nurse executives need to monitor and participate in the development of tools to support an informed patient as partner. Measurements used for improving performance can also be used to inform and educate the public. For example, the implementation of Agency for Health Care Policy and Research (AHCPR) guidelines for pressure ulcers not only reduced the incidence of pressure ulcers in one health system but also substantially reduced costs, demonstrated accountability to the public for improved outcomes, and provided a vehicle for patients and families to effectively manage their own care.

Tools themselves are not to be confused with relationships and partnerships; they support the sharing of information with consumers to guide choices as a start to building partnerships. They exemplify a willingness and accountability to enter into informed conversations with patients and members.

Summary

As new models of health care emerge and there is increased competition in the field, the ability to establish meaningful partnerships with patients is an essential capability. Failure to establish relationships and partnerships will reduce both organizations' ability to provide customer-driven, value-added care and services and their opportunities to achieve results.

Society—either as individuals or as demographic groups, populations, and communities—is telling providers that it expects clinical excellence and requires partnerships. Partnerships provide information and support and encourage patient participation in decision making about health and treatment decisions and in creating services, products, and benefit determinations. Partnering is the basis of advancing quality of care and fulfilling the obligation of caring for patients.

Partnering with patients also means partnering with the community to understand the complexities of access, community functioning, and support networks. This knowledge is essential to enter the multiple-community collaborative partnerships needed to care for the growing population of aging individuals with one or more chronic health conditions.

Acquiring and using customer knowledge is the basis for service excellence and competitive advantage. Those nurse executives and health care organizations that are knowledgeable, skilled, and committed to developing effective, sustained partnerships are those that will succeed.

References

1. Beckham, J. D. The most important day. *Healthcare Forum* 39(3):84–87, 89, May–June 1996.

2. Gerteis, M., and others. *Through the Patient's Eyes.* San Francisco: Jossey-Bass, 1993.

3. Interview with Lawrence Vander Post. *Exemplary Personalities.* Video. Topanga, CA: Human Dynamics International, 1994.

4. Morath, J. Thoughts on ethics and the art, science, and business of health care. *Allina Medical Journal* p. 6, Dec. 1996.

5. Hornberger, J. C., Habraken, H., and Bloch, D. Minimum data needed in patient preferences for accurate, efficient medical decision making. *Medical Care* 33(3):297–310, 1995.

6. Lewis, J. R.. Patient views in quality care in general practice: literature review. *Social Sciences Medicine* 39(5):655–70, 1994.

7. Morath, J., Thoughts on ethics, p. 7.

8. Deber, R. B. Physicians in healthcare management: the patient–physician partnership. Decision making, problem solving, and the desire to participate. *Canadian Medical Association Journal* 151(4):423–27, 1994

9. Vickery, D. M., and Lynch, W. D. Demand management: enabling patients to use medical care appropriately. *Journal of Emergency Medicine* 37(5), May 1995.

10. Vickery and Lynch, Demand management.

11. Kasper, J. F., Mulley, A. G., and Wennberg, J. E. Developing shared decision-making programs to improve the quality of health care. *Quality Review Bulletin* 183–90, June 1992.

12. Vickery and Lynch, Demand management.

13. Baumgarten, J. D. How will consumers use report cards in selecting health plans? *Managed Care Quarterly* 3(4):32–35, 1995.

Chapter 6

A Case Study:
Practical Partnerships

Ann Watkins, RN, BSN

Over the past six years, staff and leaders of an intensive care unit (ICU) at Abbott Northwestern Hospital in Minneapolis, MN, have applied the principles of patient–caregiver partnerships to design and build a new ICU. The unit was one component of a major innovation initiative funded in part by the Robert Wood Johnson/Pew Charitable Trusts grant entitled, "Strengthening Hospital Nursing: A Program to Improve Patient Care." The ICU project had two primary goals: (1) to improve the clinical care process for the long-term, critically ill patient with a length of stay of more than three days; and (2) to improve the support and service processes of care through the redesign of functions and roles. This case study describes the partnership principles detailed throughout this book in action at the site of care.

The Power of the Patient's Words

The patient care vision that directed the design of the new ICU, a new care delivery model and clinical process, and improvements in the care of long-term critically ill patients was inspired by the opinions of the patients themselves. Patients and family members were asked to participate in a number of focus groups, and what they told the ICU staff in those initial focus groups profoundly affected all future improvement efforts.

The focus group participants gave the following comments about the physical space in the existing ICU:

- "Patients are too crowded."
- "Nurses can't get around."
- "Nurses often bump into the bed of one patient when tending to the other."
- "Patients lose privacy and can't get rest."
- "It's noisy."
- "The temperature was too cold."

- "The closets are filled with equipment."
- "There wasn't enough room for clothes or personal belongings."

Family members were specific and articulate about what critically ill patients needed in the physical environment to feel comfortable and safe so they could direct their energy toward healing.

Through direct statements and poignant stories, patients and families made it clear that the current ICU environment was no longer workable, that hospital systems were cumbersome and disruptive, and that relationships with caregivers—the cornerstone of security for them—could be enhanced best through improved communication and care coordination. In eloquent descriptions of their experiences, participants indicated that, although they felt cared for and believed caregivers and other staff were competent, they were concerned about the coordination of care. One family member said, "The communication among the specialists (physicians) was not good. Each doctor independently was okay, but I had to initiate care conferences and ask, 'What are our goals?' The doctors made me feel like asking, 'Do we need this?' I was emotionally exhausted. It was hard to have to take on the management of the team of physicians."

Others wondered if caregivers ever talked to each other. Another family member stated, "I would think, what would happen to families who did not have the initiative, who think everything will work out eventually?" The patients themselves were telling staff partnerships were needed. The descriptive power of the patients' and families' stories challenged staff to confront the reality of care realistically through the patients' eyes.

Nurses, as caregivers, had a primary philosophy that grounded their thinking about patient care delivery. The nursing department philosophy at Abbott Northwestern Hospital states, "Patients are valued as individuals who have knowledge and information unique to themselves, a potential for self care and control over their own health decisions." Although the philosophy states that caregivers value patients as the ultimate decision makers, they were unclear about how to put that philosophy into practice.

Like most caregivers who work in an ICU setting, the staff of the existing ICU were convinced that they knew what was best for patients. With the grant's support, the staff were able to take a deeper look at patient needs. As the work began, the stories the staff heard from multiple focus groups started them on a long journey of examining their most sacredly held beliefs about ICU care and eventually led them to build an ICU that was based on the express needs of patients and families rather than their own paradigms.

The uncensored views of patients and families as they described how caregivers' actions had affected them moved ICU staff to create a vision written from the patient's perspective. (See figure 6-1.) Ledford and others state that a compelling vision statement helps make a corporate philosophy real.[1]

Figure 6-1. Station 20 Vision for Patient Care

As a patient or family member on Station 20, I can expect the following:

- My admission is centralized on Station 20 and treatment is initiated immediately.
- Upon transfer, I am confident my needs will continue to be met.
- My environment will ensure my privacy, be quiet, clean, and large enough to accommodate my family.
- I will be safe and feel secure in my surroundings.
- My care team will be accessible and consistent, competent, and reliable throughout my stay.
- State-of-the-art diagnostics and treatments will be available for me and used judiciously.
- I am confident my rights will be explained and my decisions respected.
- A person who knows my wishes will act on my behalf if I am unable to make my own decisions.
- Everyone who interacts with me will treat me and my family in a caring, sensitive manner.
- All information necessary for me to understand my illness and treatments will be provided.
- Everyone who interacts with me displays confidence in and respect for one another.
- My bill is accurate, understandable, and processed by the hospital on my behalf.

Source: Intensive Care Unit, Robert Wood Johnson/PEW Memorial Trust Grant Group, Abbott Northwestern Hospital, 1990.

When the vision was first introduced to nurses and physicians, many were aghast. Caregivers said publicly, "This is nirvana," and "You can't show this to patients. They'll start to expect this level of care." Four years later, nurses preparing for a Joint Commission on Accreditation of Healthcare Organizations survey requested that the same vision statement be hung on the wall, next to the vending machines, and across from the visitor restrooms. They had come a long way from their original fear of accountability to engage in partnerships and shape care delivery decisions with the patient and family.

Based on the vision statement, those who participated in its creation came to believe some basic tenets of ICU design:

- The patient's room is his or her sanctuary.
- Families and visitors should always be welcome and respected.
- Supplies and equipment must be located where the work is performed.
- Space for partnership among patients, families, and caregivers is essential for care planning and decision making.

In essence, the environment itself must be therapeutic.

The new physical environment of the ICU needed to bridge the gap between the reality of a 24-bed, 8,500-square-foot ICU with semiprivate rooms, a crowded waiting area, and limited conference space, and the vision of a new ICU that patients and families had created with the staff. Creating an environment that would make the vision of the ideal patient care experience real became a unifying force for creating a physical environment conducive to partnership.

A design team consisting of unit staff, physicians, professional colleagues, and stakeholders from other departments volunteered to tackle the task of closing the gap between current reality and the vision. The ICU design team members set out to build an ICU with an environment in which patients could meet their goals for healing, and caregivers could support patients' care plans with ease. All ICU staff members were determined to live out their vision for care in their decision making and actions. This process tested the degree to which caregivers were open to listening to what patients and family members had to say. In chapter 1 of this book, Robert Jeddeloh describes listening as essential to the partnership process. That is true. It also often turns out to be more difficult than anticipated.

For example, in planning the construction of the ICU, each time a major hurdle — such as assigning square footage to rooms — occurred, patients and families were consulted for a reality check about the decision's impact on them and on care delivery. These consultations highlighted the difficulties staff had with making the transition to a real partnership with patients.

Including Families in the Patient Care Process

One instance in which staff planning proved contrary to patient and family wishes was in the accommodations (both physical and procedural) made for families for visiting. The staff spent extensive time reviewing research studies that indicated what families and patients needed when they were in the ICU. After studying the literature and making site visits to other ICUs, the design team and architects carefully placed the family lounge at the back of the unit where a huge bank of windows was located. Natural lighting, they had learned, was critical to family members' ability to cope with the crisis of having a loved one in the ICU and to make important decisions regarding the patient's care. The design of the lounge was intended to provide what the literature said families needed — a quiet comfortable area with lots of light. They used an expert model in planning, using existing evidence from the literature and their professional opinions.

The moment of truth came when family members asked why, in the design plans, the family lounge was located so far away from the patient rooms. They told the design team the lounge needed to be located in the center of the unit, where they would feel close to their loved ones and where they could more easily see physicians as they made rounds. Compared with maintaining a feeling of inclusion in the care process and a partnership with caregivers, natural lighting was a much less critical factor in the design of the waiting area.

Nurses, on the other hand, had two disparate reasons for wanting the family lounge at the back of the unit: (1) to meet family members' aesthetic and biorhythmic needs for a calm, welcoming lounge; and (2) to separate family members from the patients so the nurses could do their work. Physicians wanted the lounge in the back of the unit so they could avoid meeting family members before they had a chance to review patients' progress. In some cases, the physicians wanted to avoid family members altogether until discussions could be held in a controlled situation.

In the end, the building group decided to change the plans to reflect the family members' wishes. The desire was to model behavior that made the patient and family the primary source of information on which health care decisions—including the building of an ICU—were based and to make families central to the patient care process by placing the ICU waiting room symbolically at the center of the unit. If the design team wanted caregivers to interact with patients and families as true partners, they needed to set the standard with the physical environment.

The next step was to make the family lounge a place where family members felt welcome, as partners should. In the traditional ICU setting, family members were encouraged to go home, and every effort was made to create an environment that dissuaded family members from spending extended periods of time in the ICU. The old lounge was located outside of the unit; was decorated with cheap, uncomfortable hotel furniture; and had no private space.

In many ICUs, space for family members has a low priority, but focus group participants told the design team that having a family member in the ICU signified a crisis to them, and that one of their greatest needs was to remain near that family member. After listening to participants' experiences, the team responded by creating a large family lounge, decorated with soothing colors and artwork, and equipped with a saltwater aquarium; plants; two private, quiet rooms for reflection, consultation, or grieving; a kitchen/dining area; a TV/VCR; lockers; a cupboard stocked with pillows, blankets, and toiletries; and recliners and other comfortable seating.

The design team realized that no matter how comfortable the surroundings, the care experience would not feel like a real partnership if the artificial barrier of visiting hours was still present to keep families at arm's length. Although staff members made slow strides toward easing limitations in the unit's visiting policy, a sign outside the unit clearly explained the specific (and still restrictive) visiting rules. As a result of family-member input, staff members decided the sign in the new ICU would read, "Visiting is determined by patient needs."

Consideration of Patient Needs in Unit Construction

At the heart of the design project were large, private patient rooms, which were arranged in four clusters of six rooms in a half circle around a central patient care station. Each cluster had a large oval table that could be used for patient care review and caregiver-to-caregiver consultation. Full-length glass doors were selected for patient rooms after talking with patients who explained that the security of being able to see their nurses was as important as being able to see outdoors. The staff members' discovery process about what would really work for patients, families, and front-line staff repeated itself over and over throughout the design period as the dialogue continued.

The focus on patients as the staff's most important partners manifested itself in a number of elements in the unit's construction. Staff members knew and patients and families validated that the nurse–patient relationship was key to the patient's sense of security and ability to mobilize his or her inner resources for healing. Each element of the unit's design was built around the patients to maximize the amount of time nurses spent with them. Services, equipment, and care were centered around the patient's bedside. Also included in the design was the Point of Care computerized patient record. Locating terminals in patient rooms allowed caregivers to remain in closer proximity to the patient while entering data, thus improving data accuracy, the patient's ability to participate in care, and the patient's and family's overall relationships with care providers.

Having worked in an environment that provided every possible obstacle to partnership, staff members knew that physical surroundings play an important role in supporting collaborative relationships with patients and families. The complexity of the unit's patient population required interactive planning among caregivers from multiple disciplines and with family members. For patients to progress through their episode of illness, it was essential to generate a solid plan of care to meet patients' and families' needs in a timely, compassionate, and cost-effective manner. Thus, each patient care area had space built in to allow for conferences, in addition to two separate meeting rooms.

In August 1993, the new 24-bed medical/surgical/neurological ICU opened. Fundamental to the ICU design—and to the continuing work of the unit staff—was another statement from the nursing department philosophy: "Patients are the reason we exist." During the unit's open house, those involved in the design invited the rest of the hospital to share in the unit's opening. Patients and family members who participated in the planning had the honor of cutting the ribbon.

Beyond the Physical Structure: A Model for Patient–Family–Caregiver Partnership

At Abbott Northwestern, the ICU staff and hundreds of others from throughout the hospital learned that having a vision is the key to effective unit design.

The customer must be the primary focus of that vision. It is essential to ask patients and families what they want and then do it. What they have learned since is that, although the physical construction of a unit may require that partnerships be established, moving those partnerships forward is a complex and ongoing process.

Jack, the son of a patient in the old ICU, participated in the patient/family focus groups to review the plans for the new ICU. In the middle of one discussion, Jack asked the group, "Did any of you have issues around communication when you or your family member were in the ICU?" Such issues among caregivers and with families had surfaced repeatedly during the design process.

In chapter 2, Carol Huttner and Rickie Ressler state that patients' direct access to information is critical to the success of demand management. Although the ICU's physical environment was designed to support partnerships, that could not ensure that meaningful communication would occur. Regardless of the setting, the degree to which family members felt they received necessary information was inconsistent. Variables such as the family's desire for participation, the caregiver's understanding of the family's perspective, how much value the caregiver saw in family participation, and other factors affected the ability to form partnerships.

Recently, staff in the ICU have begun testing a process of holding a family conference within the first two days of admission to the ICU. The conference is followed by another conference on day 7 and day 14, depending on the patient's course. Caregivers immediately begin to talk with family members about the possible scenarios in which the patient might find himself or herself. In this way, family members have the opportunity to begin to think about what they would do in each of the possible scenarios and to prepare themselves through rehearsal of their options.[2]

A progress note in the computerized patient record is used to give all caregivers a common understanding of what has been discussed and decided. Included in the note are prompts to clarify key aspects of care and the family's response. Progress notes double as a guide for ongoing talks with families and as documentation of the discussions. These notes should decrease the fragmentation that patients and families spoke about in the focus groups when they asked, "Don't you [physicians and other caregivers] ever talk with each other?"

Talking about possible contingencies and developing relationships with families has improved the quality of the care experience for the patient. Fundamental to the process is the idea that patients, families, and individual providers need to partner with one another. Intangible but crucial elements such as trust and mutual understanding need to be developed for both groups to appreciate the partnership. The success of this process will be measured and monitored using information from the Picker Institute's satisfaction survey instrument, which focuses on relevant dimensions of care.

The complexity issue Bryan Bushick describes in chapter 3 is real. Subsequent improvement activities surrounding patient and family involvement in planning and decision making underscore Bushick's assertion that although patients appear to be highly interested in obtaining information about their condition and options, they have less interest in actually assuming full decision-making responsibility. This scenario varies depending on the individuals involved, but in general Abbott Northwestern's ICU staff have found that family members seek varying levels of information and want their caregivers to assist them with making decisions. The level of a family member's interest rests neither with the "physician-knows-best" scenario, in which a physician's instructions are followed without question, nor with a scenario from the other end of the spectrum in which they are left all to themselves in making critical decisions. The answer lies in a balance of the two scenarios.

Caregivers need refined assessment skills to determine patients' and family members' desires and to sense changes in those desires for participation in planning and decision making. ICU staff have been exploring a formal mechanism for assessing a family's and patient's values systems. This mechanism includes a chaplain who is involved in planning and decision making and who can assess, advocate, and clarify the patient's and family's values throughout the hospital stay. This values clarification work will augment the process of scenario building.

It will be very important for caregivers to develop skills to work with patients and family members as they make decisions to avoid what Bushick calls the "one-size-fits-all" phenomenon. Unit staff could end up shirking their responsibility for assisting patients and family members with decision making under the guise that making the decision is the sole responsibility of the patient. This would be just as easy as when staff made decisions largely without consulting the patient or family member in the past. Ultimately, the practitioner's role is much more sophisticated than either of these extremes. In reality, physicians and nurses cannot know precisely what will happen to the patient physically or precisely what his or her response will be either to the event that brought him or her to the ICU or to the recovery or health status alterations that follow. The caregiver, then, must be expert at listening to the fears, values, goals, and aspirations of the patient and family, and working with them through the uncertainties of a crisis. Many patients and families currently experience inconsistency from caregivers. Some individual providers have been naturally partnering with patients throughout their careers, whereas others have difficulty in even raising important subjects with patients and family members.

An Improvement Strategy Focuses on Practical Application

Since the opening of the new ICU in 1993, practitioners, support staff, and leaders have experienced a variety of system changes designed to foster patient and family participation. In the early days of implementing such changes, it seemed that everything was a vast and complex project. Staff members and physicians from all over the hospital were involved in the design and planning process, and funds were available from the Robert Wood Johnson/Pew Memorial Trust grant and from the hospital to finance changes. It was easy to be partners when the projects were large and the pockets were deep. In recent years, however, resources for major projects have become scarce. Staff and physicians, pushed hard by the challenges of caring for the critically ill with decreasing reimbursement, now want practical improvements rather than grandiose-sounding projects.

The vision for patient-centered care and an ICU designed to support partnerships slowly became one part of a series of strategies to improve patient care for long-term, critically ill patients. In their partnerships with patients and their families, providers learned from those early focus groups that families were faced with a variety of tough decisions. For long-term ICU patients, being in the ICU was a life-changing experience, making them a perfect target for improvement efforts.

For this purpose, staff members worked to create "practical partnerships," collaborative relationships among practitioners based on a realistic approach to the issues at hand rather than an idealistic view of what partnerships should be. Practitioners joined an Institute for Health Care Improvement collaborative made up of ICU physicians, nurses, and other caregivers from across the country and learned the model of "guerrilla improvement."[3] In this model, all partners who make valuable contributions to the care process decide to take action to fix a problem.

In the ICU, the team wishes to decrease delays in advancing care for the long-term ICU patient. Staff members take on only as much as they can implement from one Tuesday to the next. Using this strategy, caregivers in the ICU have implemented protocols for management of agitation and management of nutrition, guidelines for the care of the dying patient, a conferencing/communication process for helping families and patients make critical decisions, and a written guide for family conferences and communication.

Staff members have refined a strategy of work-group participation that gets physicians and other key caregivers together to develop, agree on, and use guidelines. Because they are working on an issue uniquely relevant to their practice, work-group members make quick decisions and, in the tradition of the rapid improvement model, decide to try only as many solutions as they can begin to test within a few days. They implement the new idea, get feedback, amend the design, and try again until it seems to work right; then, they stop. Physicians in particular say they like this model because they can drop in and out of the process—they feel included and yet are not forced to engage in what they perceive as a never-ending committee. They can be partners without committing to months of participation.

This process has also resulted in less resistance to change. Searching for "better" rather than "best" practices gives work-group members more license for creative action and arouses less fear at not "getting it perfect." A staff nurse new to the ICU in the past year recently stated that she had no idea there was a big project under way to improve the care of long-term ICU patients. She was, however, able to describe in detail the individual initiatives and to tell stories about the patients with whom she had used various protocols and guidelines. She also said that, although her colleagues knew and talked about the improvements among themselves, she believed that most of them didn't know it was a big project. In her words, this was "some of the most practical stuff" she had seen accomplished in a long time.

This improvement process has significantly increased staff members' ability to change practice quickly. They no longer try for perfection, they try for improvement. They no longer seek partnerships of a particular scope and length of participation, they build partnerships with shared goals and time limits on the work in which they're involved. Resistance to change has decreased because each step is performed in small, meaningful increments and in real time. The emphasis is on action and implementation, not training or education. The work group relies on the attractive force of a good idea to spread commitment from caregiver to caregiver. Their partnerships are built on a foundation of clarity of purpose and shared accomplishments.

Barriers to Partnership: Valuing Individual Contributions

Barbara Balik's descriptions in chapter 4 of how to develop partnerships with patients and families, as well as the levels of partnership, are interesting when considered in context with the case study of this ICU. Unit staff have had a great deal of exposure to ideas pertaining to partnerships with patients and families. They have made changes in their approach to family visiting issues and to families' involvement in planning and decision making regarding patients. Still, they have not moved beyond a family-focused model. Caregivers have an increased degree of collaboration with family members and patients, while at the same time continuing in the role of caregiver as advisor and guide. They don't yet think of themselves as agents of the patient and family. Fear of losing control and mutual dependence on one another—both for the customer and agent—are at the heart of this issue. Relationships seem to be the key.

In the ICU, caregivers have made some progress in understanding how they function in relation to one another. There appear to be some prerequisites (such as recognizing one's own contribution and understanding the role of other caregivers and support staff) that are necessary before staff members can move into true partnerships with patients and family members. For example, three years ago, staff nurses on the unit became agitated when plans to hire multiskilled workers to do housekeeping and nurse's aide tasks reached the implementation stage. Though it appeared at first that their concerns were entirely centered on the patient-support issue, there was actually a pervasive lack of respect between staff levels. This situation was aggravated by many nurses' inability to clearly articulate how their work differed from that of aides. Although they understood the difference instinctively, they couldn't share it with others. Essentially, they were hesitant to enter a partnership because they were unable to explain why their contribution was necessary and unique.

The work group embarked on a process to clarify the scope of professional nursing practice for ICU nurses. Stories were sought and celebrated as a means of identifying themes that described the richness of the nurses' work. Through these stories, staff members were able to move beyond a list of tasks that nurses performed toward an understanding of their real work, including the elements of the nursing process and the critical nature of developing relationships with patients and their families in care planning. Both the art and science of nursing in the ICU became apparent when the nurses were able to give voice to the depth of their contributions. Anxiety decreased among the nursing staff as they came to view their roles as distinct from those of other support staff, such as nursing assistants and unit secretaries. This kind of clarity has and will let them establish partnerships with greater ease.

The introduction of multiskilled employees into the ICU also highlighted another phenomenon. Some staff members remained somewhat aloof during the process, watching from a distance and expecting it to fail. Some admitted their attitudes were based on the bias that people who worked as aides didn't have the capacity to learn and perform multiple functions effectively. Soon after the new employees started, an interesting change began to occur. Once ICU personnel got to know the new employees, the tone of resistance changed. "Those people will never be able to do that level of prioritization," became "Oh, sure, Jane and Carl and Susan can do it easily, but that's because they are who they are. Another person wouldn't be able to perform the same role." Staff members learned that once they entered into relationships with one another, it became increasingly difficult to dislike and diminish others' abilities. They knew each other as individuals and had begun to develop trust, the essential foundation for a strong partnership. The checklist for exchanging information in chapter 4 might be applied to relationships among provider employees. As institutions move toward including patients and families in their partnerships, work on internal partnerships must continue as well.

Summary

When patients and families spoke to the ICU staff in the focus groups, the message was clear: They wanted partnerships. The staff embraced the voice of the patient and family and brought the customer into the process. The customer's voice is what Julianne Morath refers to as the cornerstone of patient care quality. The ICU staff members and leaders built the physical structure to support partnerships and found that, while essential, physical space and ambience alone didn't create partnerships with patients and families, or even among staff. Relationships which honor the patient's and family members' changing desire for partnership and which value the contribution of unique caregivers are necessary to create meaningful partnership. The biggest discovery for the group is that, even if caregivers can get past their own personal mental models, generating practical health care improvements in today's market is difficult because of the complexity of assessing what is right for any one patient and family.

References

1. Ledford, G. E., Wendenhof, J. R., and Strahley, J. T. Realizing a corporate philosophy. *Organizational Dynamics* 11, Winter 1995.

2. Moldow, G., Veterans Administration, Minneapolis, MN. July 1996. Personal communication.

3. Berwick, D. *Adult ICU Breakthrough Collaborative.* Institute for HealthCare Improvement. Boston, April 1996.

Keeping the Promise: Redefining Health Care into the 21st Century

Gordon M. Sprenger, MHA

Those of us who have focused our lifelong career energies on health care delivery and systems might take a cynical view as we read the title of this third book in the series published by American Hosptal Publishing for the American Organization of Nurse Executives—*Patient as Partner: The Cornerstone of Community Health Improvement.* After all, hasn't the patient always been our primary health care partner?

Unfortunately for all of us, the truthful answer is "no." Patients have not always been our partners, and we as care providers have too often fallen short in partnering with them. We have built facilities without asking patients how their experience could be enhanced by patient-driven modifications to our hospitals and clinics. We have provided care with expectations of little patient interference, and we too often have provided information on a "need-to-know" basis. Our approach has been kindly, parental, and all-knowing, in the spirit of benevolent dictatorships. Whether physicians, nurses, or hospital administrators, we knew best. We were the experts.

We are still experts; we have worked hard to be so and we have much to offer when we work to relieve human suffering, to improve health, and at the minimum to do no harm. But today we see the maturing of an essential element in how we approach, design, and do our work. That element is the patient as partner. And full patient partnership, especially in efforts to improve community health, will shape the health care system of the future.

I mention a health care system, yet I believe the most daunting challenge we face is to explode the myth that we have a health care system in this country. Those of us who provide expertise and care know that we have a fragmented "system." We have a hospital system, a public health system, physician systems, financing systems, insurance systems, and so on. All these separate systems together make up the overall health care system. But it is fragmented,

Portions of the epilogue appeared as part of Mr. Sprenger's investiture speech as president of the American Hospital Association, Jan. 28, 1996.

and many times the pieces don't work together very well. They duplicate each other and, in the end, don't serve patients nearly as well as they could.

For example, my mother is 88 and her health care is paid for largely through Medicare and a commercial (Blue Cross) supplemental plan. She lives in a rural Minnesota community, goes to the local hospital when necessary, and receives routine care from a family practice physician in town. For specialty care, she travels 75 miles north to the Minneapolis metropolitan area, after which she convalesces in my family home in Minneapolis. She then returns to her rural community, her hometown physician, and local hospital, assisted by a public health nurse and a home care aide who help her live independently in her own home.

Now, as a long-time hospital and health care administrator, I am close to the system and I am someone who believes that by and large the "system" delivers good care. But, do I believe there's a system of health care to take care of my mother? Not really, not in the sense of a true care continuum. Is there anyone I can hold accountable for her care? Yes, at different points. And I suspect that at each point some effort is made to include her in the decision making for her own care as a partner. But no one is really accountable for her care in terms of an integrated approach. There is no single person or place (care provider or financing organization) to whom I can turn to be certain that her health is maintained at the highest possible level. In most cases, the financial side of health care is divorced from the delivery side, and the delivery side is fragmented within itself.

Fortunately, those of us "on the inside" can help our aging parents navigate through this system. But for many people, including just about anyone without health care experience or whose life circumstances result in significant barriers to ready access (poverty, illiteracy, chronic illness, language barriers), there are few advocates to help them traverse these multiple systems. If we are going to change this situation, we must create new definitions.

First, we need a whole new definition of partnership, whether between hospitals and managed care organizations, between alternative therapies and the traditional health care model, between for-profit and nonprofit entities, between us and our communities. And of course, we need new, effective partnerships between patients and those who care for them, whether in the hospital, at home, in the clinic, or in a long-term care facility. The partnership must be change making, breaking down barriers of incomprehensibility and complexity in a system that is designed to serve patients. As components of the "system", we must partner and listen.

Certainly, a new definition of responsibility is needed. It is not enough for us to be leaders of the old hierarchical health care organizations of the past. We must take responsibility for new community care networks that bring the fragmented system together and embrace a health improvement model.

If we indeed move from a model focused on illness and injury to one focused on community health, accountability will be defined differently. And this shift could be disconcerting as we seek a new balance with patients as partners. After all, partners are empowered and their fully informed decisions must be respected. A fully informed, empowered patient may make decisions that make us uncomfortable—with the process, with the priorities, and even with the outcome. To find a balance in our new role and in a new kind of accountability will require focus and time.

Finally, the definition of results must change, particularly for the people we serve. A positive clinical outcome may be lacking in many ways without the full psychosocial spectrum of discovery and action that results from partnering with patients. Our definition of "customer" must broaden to include many interrelated communities, such as enrolled health plan members, employer groups, and special needs groups such as the elderly and the poor.

These new definitions present tremendous challenges and offer complex opportunities. Let me raise some questions. How do we understand and meet community health needs when most of us have been focused on acute care, which is how in many cases we are reimbursed (often hardly enough to comfortably do that task)? Who will pay for these essential partnerships, for the work of community health improvement?

Can we "insiders" create these new definitions of partnership, responsibility, accountability, and results? Can we alone take the fragmented systems of today and create something new for tomorrow? No, we can't. This is work that must be done by entire communities with physicians and patients as partners and with the full involvement of public health systems, school systems, social service agencies, and all levels of government. We must listen, ask questions, listen some more, and act on our information to achieve our seamless community care model. With that model in place, we can then approach the financing systems—insurance companies, HMOs, government agencies—and build the right incentives into a new risk–reward relationship that should pay for the new integrated, health-focused model.

What can happen when we reach out and engage our community, when we ask those we serve to be true partners in the design and delivery of care? Recently, in a rural Minnesota town, there was a meeting with a school nurse, a principal, a school superintendent, the police chief, a city councilman, a Protestant minister, the hospital administrator, a nurse, and a physician. They were asked what they could do to make their community healthier. In typical small-town style, they looked at each other and concluded that they didn't have any problems. Then the school nurse interceded: "Let's be real. Last week, I saw three high school girls, unwed and pregnant, who live in this community. This is a problem."

Under the old definition of responsibility, the hospital administrator, the nurse, and the physician would have focused on getting the young women into prenatal care. But the new definitions and the interdisciplinary group at the table resulted in the discussion taking a different turn. They discussed why teenage pregnancies were on the rise and whether there was a way for the group to make a difference in young people's lives and prevent teen pregnancy. They learned that most teenage sex occurs between 3:00 and 5:00 PM among kids who are not involved in supervised after-school activities. The principal talked about why some students are disenfranchised from extracurricular activities; the chief of police cited problems caused by unsupervised students after school; and of course prenatal care for the young women was discussed.

The rich discussion centered on the core problems of the situation rather than just the health issues. In this era of severely constrained financial resources, the only way to deal with some health care issues will be to solve some of our social problems. I urge those who work in health care to create partnerships with their communities to address violence, youth problems, unemployment, and housing with the same vigor used to attack illness.

Today, the health care community stands on the river bank. We save people after they've fallen from the boat and have been swept downstream. We often perform great medical miracles to accomplish these rescues. But unless we journey up the river and find out why they have fallen out of the boat in the first place, we will never have enough resources to save everyone who washes downstream. I am not suggesting that we can take on all the social and public health problems of the world. However, I truly believe that we can leverage our communities' limited resources much more effectively than we can leverage resources in our individual health care organizations.

What is this new system we are moving toward? Take as an example one of our ambulance drivers in the Minneapolis area who recently responded to a 911 call at a senior citizen's home. The call said that a woman had fallen and broken her hip. On arrival, the driver found that her hip was not broken and that she was frightened but substantially all right. After helping her up and calming her, he looked around to find that her home was in disarray with objects scattered on the floors and stairs. In addition, the woman had severe arthritis, so she could not bend to pick up fallen objects. What he saw was a disaster waiting to happen. Although she hadn't broken her hip this time, the chances were very great that she soon would.

Under the old definition of responsibility, the driver would have taken the woman to a hospital emergency room. She would have gone to radiology, where x-rays would have confirmed that her hip was not broken, and she would have been sent home. After all, if a worker is in the transportation and/or hospital business, providing service is the only way to get reimbursed.

But in this case, a new definition of responsibility led to a glimpse of a new, integrated system. The woman is a member of a Medicare health plan, part of an integrated community care network that is totally responsible— medically and financially—for her health. The ambulance driver called the network's home health agency, which sent an aide to clean and help the woman organize her home for easier and safer access. The specter of a future broken hip diminished greatly.

Where all this takes us, I believe, is to our vision of community health care networks through partnerships—serving populations and being held accountable for their health status. This vision is only possible if we see ourselves assuming more responsibility and accountability and not just as "for rent" when our services are needed.

As we move forward into a new environment with new definitions and new expectations, we have one more enormous challenge to confront—our own past. The future can best be shaped by holding onto the best of the past. It is rather like moving to a new home; it takes wisdom to know what you should load up and take with you and what you should put out at the garage sale. In many respects, that's where we are in health care today. What things in health care do we need to leave behind as we move into the future? With what do we replace these archaic beliefs, systems, and methods? I believe the future will result in less focus on bricks and mortar, and more on programs. We will be working to develop opportunities to better manage the health plan premium dollar for new resource allocations. We will look at the historical medical staff structure and at ways we can economically partner with our physicians. It will mean leaving empty the wing that really isn't needed or converting it to a day care center.

We must take financial risk more than ever before. We must ask fundamental questions about what services are needed, how they are designed, and for whom. Our accountability and responsibility demands that we maximize scarce resources. We cannot tolerate duplication, and we must eliminate any truth in the statement that 30 percent of what health care professionals do is not needed. We also must push to change the incentives to true health care rather than ill care.

We must move swiftly to establish clinical care models that reflect best demonstrated practices. And we must keep asking the tough questions and listening to the answers provided by one of our key partners: patients.

It is also vital that we recapture our communities' trust in what we do and how we do it. Historically, communities have looked to health care organizations as havens of safety and caring. Is that image tainted today? Polls from communities around the country tell us we need to spruce up our image. Some say providers are more interested in the financial solvency of the individuals presenting for treatment than with their needs. It is essential that we earn back community trust during this transformation if we are going to provide leadership to move to the new models. Engaging patients as partners could be the first step.

The next five years promise to be a watershed that clearly delineates one era of American health care from another—a change as dramatic as Lyndon Johnson introducing Medicare in the 1960s. The old ways will no longer work. The lesson for us? Breakthroughs are required—and time is growing short. The public is crying for a more responsible, accountable, outcome-focused, partner-driven, collaborative system.

We need a burst of the same managerial imagination and audacity that created the American heritage of which we are so proud: the best health care in the world. That same kind of health care leadership of the past—imaginative, risk-taking, patient-sensitive, community-based leadership—will be needed even more in the future if we are going to keep our promise of meeting community needs, of taking care of people, through community partnerships that are accountable, responsible, and results focused.

Oliver Wendell Holmes, who was a physician as well as an author, once said, "The mind—stretched to a new idea—never goes back to its original dimension." That is, indeed, what is happening in the field of health care today. We cannot go back to what it was. In our communities, we are creating new definitions of care and forming new ideas from old words and old ways. As a result, we are seeing new partnerships that include patients and communities. We are seeing our roles change with new responsibilities. We are exhibiting renewed accountability for who and what we are. And we are focusing on new results. Once redefined—once the words are stretched into new meanings—our actions will never be the same again.